Anxiety Breakthrough

BREAKOUT OF FEAR, BREAKTHROUGH TO FREEDOM

Emotional Mastery Program

Peg Haust-Arliss, LCSW-R

Anxiety Breakthrough

BREAKOUT OF FEAR, BREAKTHROUGH TO FREEDOM

A Holistic and Integrative Approach for
Stress, Panic, and Anxiety

It's Time to Rise and Shine!

Peg Haust-Arliss, LCSW-R

BALBOA.
PRESS

A DIVISION OF HAY HOUSE

"Primary Food," "Circle of Life," and the "Integrative Nutrition Plate" designs are © Integrative Nutrition, Inc. The "Institute for Integrative Nutrition" logo design is a registered trademark of Integrative Nutrition, Inc. used with permission.

Balboa Press books may be ordered through booksellers or by contacting:

Balboa Press
A Division of Hay House
1663 Liberty Drive
Bloomington, IN 47403
www.balboapress.com
1-(877) 407-4847

Because of the dynamic nature of the Internet, any web addresses or links contained in this book may have changed since publication and may no longer be valid. The views expressed in this work are solely those of the author and do not necessarily reflect the views of the publisher, and the publisher hereby disclaims any responsibility for them.

The author of this book does not dispense medical advice or prescribe the use of any technique as a form of treatment for physical, emotional, or medical problems without the advice of a physician, either directly or indirectly. The intent of the author is only to offer information of a general nature to help you in your quest for emotional and spiritual well-being. In the event you use any of the information in this book for yourself, which is your constitutional right, the author and the publisher assume no responsibility for your actions.

Any people depicted in stock imagery provided by Thinkstock are models, and such images are being used for illustrative purposes only. Certain stock imagery © Thinkstock.

Print information available on the last page.

ISBN: 978-1-4525-7987-0 (sc)
ISBN: 978-1-4525-7989-4 (hc)
ISBN: 978-1-4525-7988-7 (e)

Library of Congress Control Number: 2013914632

Balboa Press rev. date: 3/4/2016

This book is dedicated to
all the inmates at Anxiety State Prison.
I can't wait to see you on the outside!
And to my husband, Craig, who waited patiently for my freedom.

"I honestly felt that there was no hope to ever feeling great again. I worried that I would not get back to my old self again. The help you provided really made a big difference. I noticed myself improving at an impressive rate. Peg, you taught me the tools I needed to be able to practice on my own." (CM)

"You not only gave me the tools—you taught me how to apply them. Thank you for letting me in to the world's greatest secret. How could I ever thank you enough for showing me how to take control of my life? All of my heartfelt admiration." (RY)

"I want to thank you from the bottom of my heart for helping me change my life." (KM)

"I feel confident I can do this, and I thank you for your help in making me realize that I can beat this problem. I'm in the right frame of mind." (JW)

"Coming here is one of the best decisions I ever made. I have seen progress I never knew I could achieve. I have the tools necessary to create a happier, more fulfilling life for myself and my family. I have begun running again after nearly twenty years, and I lost thirteen pounds!" (GM)

"This is the best I have ever felt about myself." (BJ)

"Meeting you was one of the best gifts life has ever bestowed upon me. Your gentle guidance and depth of knowledge have brought me to a place that I never imagined reaching again— believing that I have the power to choose how I want my life to be. From now on, I will decide what I want and then make it happen. Thank you, Peg, for helping me understand that it has always been, and always will be, *my choice*." (GL)

"Thanks so much for everything you did for me, Peg. For those without anxiety challenges it may not seem miraculous, but for me it was a miracle!" (JB)

"I can't thank you enough for helping me to find myself again. I know what it means to live my life now, and it's an amazing feeling. I'm extremely grateful that I mentioned needing 'homework' to my doctor in order to get me to wake up to the way life can be, because if I hadn't, I don't know that I would have been connected with you or be where I am now. Thank you for what you do." (JS)

"You are a gem hidden in the Finger Lakes!" (LM)

Contents

Preface

You are reading these words now because you are struggling with excessive anxiety, stress, or panic attacks. You are here to find answers, maybe for the first time or maybe after a number of attempts to find relief. You know that comparing an anxiety disorder to a prison sentence is not a big stretch. In "Anxiety State Prison" your freedoms are taken away. Freedoms that most people take for granted—such as socializing, shopping, driving, going to events, or traveling—become difficult or even impossible. The beautiful, all-encompassing world becomes small and confined to a cell. You may not be completely restricted—maybe only certain situations are avoided or tolerated, resulting in a life on parole (you're out, but with limitations)—but that is not the life you deserve! You deserve *complete* freedom!

Why did I write this book? There are some fantastic self-help books on anxiety, and I have used some of them to break out of my own anxiety prison, but a couple of things have always concerned me. First, the fact that anxiety is commonly considered a "disorder" implies that it is a disease beyond our control. Second, "Big Pharma" promotes medications as *the* answer. Before we begin this quest together, I think you should know my stance on these issues:

It is both my personal belief and my professional opinion that anxiety is *not* a disorder. I do not believe that you are in any way mentally ill if you have anxiety—or that you are powerless over it. I believe it does more harm than good to be labeled. I believe the use of medication without education and alternative options is a disservice to those struggling with stress and anxiety.

Let me be very clear. I am in no way stating that I believe mental illness does not exist. Feelings of anxiety and depression are very real and can be severe. I am also not stating that medications do not work. I know medications have been a blessing for many people. You may be proof of that yourself. And I completely believe that taking medications is a personal choice, one that I do not counsel for or against. What I *am* saying is that far too many people believe they have *no* control over what they are experiencing, and part of the problem, in my opinion, is being labeled. Once a person has been given any label, it affects their experience; the label becomes their reality. Just ask adults who were told they were "just shy" all their lives. What I tell my clients, I will tell you now: there is relief for anxiety, and as you will see, you have more power than you know. And regarding medication, if you are responsibly taking medications advised by your doctor for your anxiety or depression, and you find it helpful and do not want to discontinue, then *don't*. My intention is for you to gain new tools and strategies to get you further than you are now. If you do want to discontinue your meds, *do not do so without the supervision of your doctor*. If you are considering medications, educate yourself, research, talk with your doctor, and ask questions. Learn both how the meds can help you as well as how their effectiveness may be limited. These days, in a world of managed care, it has become our responsibility as consumers to educate ourselves on what we are taking and research all options. Make an educated decision that makes sense for you.

Through most of my career, I felt alone in my beliefs, because I was in a traditional disease model environment. But later I learned that I wasn't alone. I learned that there are psychological approaches that address the same concerns. I have embraced those approaches and combined them with time-tested and reliable traditional approaches, resulting in this book and in the Holistic Emotional Mastery programs I have created that complement this book.

My mission is to contribute to the shift that is taking place more and more all over the world—the shift from a reactive, symptom-driven, disease approach to a proactive, practical, empowering, all-natural approach.

My passion is to share the tools and strategies that I have personally used to break out of my own anxiety prison. The truth is that life is too short *and* too long to be living in a tiny little cell. Right now, as you read this, you are the oldest you've ever been *and* the youngest you will ever be. It's time for you to break out, too. I am so excited for this chance to be a part of your escape plan.

Rise and shine,
Peg

Introduction

You try to figure out what is wrong, so you go online and do extensive research. Unintentionally, you've scared yourself, because you find you have all the signs and symptoms of various serious illnesses. Now convinced that you have a serious medical condition, you go to your doctor, or maybe you show up at the ER because you fear you're having a heart attack! The doctor responsibly conducts all the necessary tests to rule out conditions and find a cause. Nothing. "All clear," they say. You then get officially diagnosed with an anxiety disorder. You say, "Anxiety? No way! This can't be anxiety. It's too serious!" You may have been told that you have an incurable condition and that, unfortunately, you will have this disorder for the rest of your life. You are told that you will just have to learn to cope. The solution? Take a pill. It's not the doctor's fault; they are treating your symptoms medically, the way they know. If you are fortunate, you have a collaborative doctor who also suggested psychotherapy, coaching, or other holistic modalities.

So, *now* how do you feel? Do you feel relief, because it means that it is real, it has a name, and others must experience it too? Do you also feel relief knowing that you have that script? Who could blame you. Or do you feel angry that they didn't find a "real cause," because this can't possibly be mind-related? Or do you feel an emotional mix: relieved and ashamed, as though somehow it's admitting to yourself that having this disorder is your fault. After all, people in your life are telling you to just "stop it," and you don't understand why you can't. Or maybe you're relieved but fearful, because you're not a "med person," but, you know, what choice do you have? Or maybe you feel relieved, fearful, and depressed, because you now believe that you will have to live with this the rest of your life.

I want to help you change all that! And here is how:

MY APPROACH

- holistic: Mind, body, and spirit. Promoting the belief that these three elements of a human being must be seen together in order to achieve any notion of healing.
- integrative: You will be exposed to tools and strategies from cognitive behavioral therapy (CBT), the most widely-used therapy for anxiety. Research has shown it to be effective in the treatment of panic, phobias, social anxiety, and generalized anxiety, among many other challenges.
  And neuro-linguistic programming (NLP), developed in the 1970s by John Grinder (a linguistics professor) and Richard Bandler (a mathematician). Through extensive research, Grinder and Bandler studied what made some therapists more effective than others. Based on their observations, a set of principles and techniques used to create change during therapy was created.
- all-natural: It requires no drugs or dangerous chemicals.
- action-oriented: Change is not just knowledge but also action; practice and journaling will move you forward consistently.
- encouraging and empowering.
- structured and disciplined: Commit to yourself; you will get out of it what you put into it.
- focused on elimination of symptoms versus management of symptoms.

You may have already tried a number of different ways to combat your anxiety, from traditional counseling, psychotherapy, and medication to nontraditional routes, such as acupuncture and other energy modalities. Natural solutions are becoming more common today. As a psychotherapist *and* health coach, I'm excited to study how food is related to our moods. There are many different schools of thought, schools of therapy, and solutions, all using their own unique treatment model.

You have probably heard the phrase "mind, body, spirit." In this book—and in all my programs—I focus on each of these areas. You can make dramatic changes in each of these areas alone, but *lasting* change comes when all three areas are nurtured. With the first key, you will unlock powerful strategies for creating the mind-set necessary to kick anxiety symptoms to the curb. With the second key, you will discover what your physical body needs for optimal emotional wellness, and with the final key, you travel far beyond just coping and managing symptoms and move upward and onward to a truly fulfilling life!

KEY #1 FREEDOM FOR YOUR MIND

Our minds are amazingly powerful. Sadly, we often sell ourselves extremely short with our negative and limited thinking. I cover tools and strategies rooted in cognitive therapy, neuro-linguistic programming (NLP), and the law of attraction. You will clearly realize that what we think is directly related to how we feel. All emotions are necessary, and I don't label them as good or bad. Instead, I look at them as muscles; we need them all, but some, in this case anxiety, can become an "overdeveloped muscle." You will learn how to have the mind-set that creates emotional strength and durability for life.

KEY #2 FREEDOM FOR YOUR BODY

What good is *emotional* fitness if you're lacking energy and feeling *physically* unfit? Have you seen those movies where the guy is stuck in prison and all he does is work out, resulting in a complete physical transformation when he's released? This book will guide you to make the necessary changes that your body needs to provide better protection and immunity and ensure that you won't be going back to your old cell any time soon.

KEY #3 FREEDOM FOR YOU!
FREEDOM AND BEYOND!

By this time you will have broken out of Anxiety State Prison. You'll be mastering your mind-set and well on your way to greater health and vitality. Moving into Key #3 will mean the difference between getting out and staying out. This is where you get your ticket to freedom forever. You will identify and rate your levels of personal growth in major life areas and then create the action plan necessary to get you there.

PART I

PREPARING FOR ESCAPE

I believe in the power of story. Stories challenge stigma. Unfortunately, many people still believe that problems with anxiety are caused by personal weakness. People often feel ashamed and want to keep their solution-seeking efforts secret. I know this stigma has no basis in reality. Stories can challenge these stigmatic beliefs and speak to the truth that there is nothing shameful about anxiety. With that, I would like to share my story with you now. Let it remind you to own who you are and to shine your unique light, courageously, with no apologies.

FEAR TO FREEDOM: MY PERSONAL STORY

Truth be known, I am a successful psychotherapist now, but never in a million years did I believe it possible to ever achieve. In fact, if someone had told me years ago that I'd be living my childhood aspirations as a successful therapist let alone a vegan health and lifestyle coach, I would have laughed.

You see, when it came to life goals, I was the girl who dreamed of going to college but was stricken with low confidence, fears, and panic. When it came to health, I could wolf down a double whopper with cheese, extra everything minus onions, large fries, and still have room for a chocolate shake. I smoked cigarettes for many years. I used to say things like: "I don't smoke cigarettes that much, and I don't want to live to be one hundred anyway!" I cringe just writing that!

Now, I'm not saying that I am perfect. Perfect is boring, and deprivation sucks! Life is about fun, and perfect is not fun! Am I now panic attack free? *Yes*! Am I a smoker? *No*! *And*, I absolutely enjoy burgers, fries, and chocolate shakes that taste *way* better than the ones I ate then.

So what happened that stopped panic attacks in their tracks and turned me completely around in how I approach life, relationships, mood, food, and even how I move?

Fast forward a few decades, a few milestone birthdays, the loss of my father and sister, tens of thousands of dollars in education, four degrees, countless certifications, the privilege of coaching hundreds of clients, and one visit to Farm Sanctuary later … I *grew*! I continue to grow. Growing keeps our spirits alive. But growth without giving is pointless and can lead to despair and anxiety. Therefore, I want to give back to you, the reader, my clients, and all who can benefit from all I have learned. Oh yes, some of it the hard way, no doubt.

Chronicles of the *Go-go-go!* Girl

Let the fears begin …

It was the night before my first day of school. I was five years old, sitting on my dad's lap. I was full of hope and joy, and I asked him if I was going to learn to read the next day. "*Yes!*" he said with an encouraging smile. "You *will* learn to read!" Dad didn't realize that I actually meant: "Daddy, will I read *fluently* when I get home tomorrow?" I couldn't contain my excitement. I was ready to *go-go-go!*

From birth to five years old I was pretty socially isolated, living in the country with lots of property, but not lots of kids. Before I entered the school system, I was surrounded by very loving parents, sisters, and fur friends. I felt loved, and everyone treated me well. I was a happy-go-lucky little girl with a very bright spirit. I was free to be authentically me.

But, then came kindergarten …

That first day was like nothing I had envisioned. Instead of learning to read, I learned I couldn't zip my zipper or tie my shoes fast enough. It looked to me like my classmates knew each other and had already established their groups. Although that was disappointing, it was nothing in comparison to what was to come: "show-and-tell." Do you remember show-and-tell? We were asked to bring our favorite toy and show it to our classmates. One Christmas, I received the best gift ever—a battery-operated dog that jumped and barked by remote control. I couldn't wait to share! The instructions were clear: form a seated circle on the floor; one at a time, stand inside the circle; state your name and where you are from, and then present your beloved toy. Easy, cool, fun! Right? Well, not so much:

"*Hi*! My name is Peggy Haust, and I live in Tyre, New York." At that moment, roaring laughter surrounded me like a vortex from the floor. "Ha-ha-ha! You live in a tire! Ha-ha-ha-ha!" It played out for me like the classic horror flick, *Carrie*. Do you remember the famous scene after she was humiliated with the bucket of blood poured on her head? "They're laughing at you! They're all laughing at you!" Although likely not the case, that was my reality. That circle became my circle of fear; they *were* all laughing at me! Not a great foundation for confidence. But kids are amazingly resilient, and by first grade I was reignited—because that was the year I *really was* going to read! Once again, I was out of my skin with excitement as we all sat on the floor facing the chalkboard to learn our first words:

"Does anyone know what this says?" my nice teacher asked. My hand flew up like a rocket reaching for the stars "*Pleeease* pick me!" Of course she picked me; she must have thought I was going to pee my pants! "*Go-go-go!*" I exclaimed with a huge smile on my face. "Yes, that's right Peggy," my teacher answered, smiling back at me. As I got a glimpse of my peers, however, they didn't seem as excited for me. To me, they had that "*Seriously*? What*ever*" look. I guess I needed to curb my enthusiasm.

I joke about it now, but what appeared as meaningless events was for me the birth of fears, phobias, and insecurities that would imprison me for many years to come. Sociologist Morris Massey has described three major life periods that influence our personalities and values.

They are:

1. the imprint period: age 0–7
2. the modeling period: age 8–13
3. the socialization period: age 13–21

The initial fear-inducing event occurred during the imprint period, a very important life stage that occurs from birth to age seven. Up until the age of seven, children are like sponges, absorbing everything around them and accepting much of it as the literal truth. Phobias tend to originate from this period, generally from ages three to seven.

Unfortunately, it can also be a time when we learn in one way or another to hide. We learn it's not okay to be our authentic selves. I, like many children, was learning to shrink and fly under the radar. Between that first *Carrie* episode in kindergarten—and its sequel in first grade—the true me, that "go-go-go girl" learned to dim her light, play small, and especially avoid public speaking at all costs.

The next stage is the modeling period, from ages eight to thirteen. Rather than taking things literally, we are modeling others and seeing if that fits for us. We begin to notice the behaviors of others around us, and we emulate our heroes. Growing up in the 1970s was absolutely inspiring, empowering, *and* confusing—because at the height of the women's movement we (men and women) received so many mixed messages. Messages from strong female leaders, icons, and role models in one ear, and societal rules, values, and expectations in the other created confusion and inner conflicts: "I am woman. Hear me *roar!*" sang Ann Murray—*but not too loud; nice girls are quiet.* "Be independent!" encouraged Gloria Steinman, *but make sure you take care of your family first.* "Want it all!" *But don't ask for much; that's greedy and selfish.* "Be smart," *but not too smart; otherwise, boys won't like you.* "Looks count," *but don't be shallow.* "Be confident," *but be careful not to seem arrogant.* I once heard it said that we become whom we most admired at the age of ten. So, armed with my Wonder Woman bracelets, knowing I could grow up to bring home the bacon, fry it up in the pan—but of course *never, never, never allow your man to forget he's a man*—away I went!

My remaining school years went fairly smoothly. There were no public speaking worries until seventh grade. This time it was sharing the Burr–Hamilton duel history project. I didn't know how to work those dang Wonder Woman bracelets! *Oh God, please get me through this.* I was in panic mode, stammering and stuttering, and I only managed to get through it by sheer disassociation. I vowed never to go through that again. I wasn't planning on going to college anyway, so I was okay with getting zeros on any projects requiring speech. One teacher offered alternate assignments. *What a great idea!* And so for the rest of high school, whenever presenting in class came up, I asked for alternative assignments.

Our life experiences and the messages we receive when we are young build our foundation and strongly influence our core beliefs. Core beliefs are our deeply held beliefs that we hold for ourselves, others, and the world. These beliefs affect how we see ourselves, the choices we make, and ultimately the results we receive in any area of life.

The socialization period, from ages thirteen to twenty-one, is another powerfully influential time. We are largely influenced by our peers and we develop relationship values. There was a time when I was in and out of a very different kind of prison—an abusive relationship. It was a constant state of anxiety, as I never knew when the next emotional or physical attack would come. Within the cycle of violence, there is calm before the storm, but in any domestic violence situation, one always has to stay on high alert. I remember the panic attacks I had while planning my first escape. I wanted to end the relationship, and I attempted this by leaving New York and moving to Florida. My cover was a two-week holiday with my sister and best friend, but my real plan was a permanent vacation. So, there I was in the back of a pickup truck at 2 a.m, me and my bestie all set up with lawn chairs, junk food, sleeping bags, and anchoring the moment with a sing-along to Bad Company's "Run With The Pack":

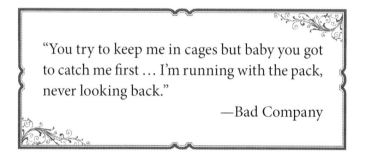

"You try to keep me in cages but baby you got to catch me first … I'm running with the pack, never looking back."

—Bad Company

I was excited about this fresh start, and I also knew the day would come when he realized I was not to return. When that happened, he came for me—and he broke the law to do it. The police were looking for him and contacted my parents to find out where I was, because they assumed that if they found me, then they would find him. They were right. I got off the phone with my parents and right away I saw him walking down the street. Scared and excited, I went outside to talk with him. Like many women, I confused drama with true love. "What happened?" I asked him. "Why are you here? How?" Once again, I chose to believe his story, whatever that was *this* time. He stayed in Florida for a while, and my parents were worried. After they caught me too many times sneaking out to meet him, my parents grounded me for the first time— from long distance! There was a part of me that didn't mind. I liked knowing my parents were taking some control when obviously I could not. Since he was in Florida, they encouraged me to go home to New

York. I obliged—and felt relief. I was home again, safe and sound, but you might be able to guess what happened next.

He turned himself in for me; at least that was the story he told me. I visited him every weekend for eight months to prove my love and loyalty. While he was locked up, I felt safe and was my free independent self. I was living life, working and enjoying friends. Since I believed that I couldn't go to college, I spent many weekends at Oswego, Potsdam, Geneseo, and Buffalo State colleges living vicariously through my friends. I joked that I got to do the fun part while they had all the work! The day of his release, I anticipated a happy reunion. I picked him up ready for a warm celebration, but instead I was received with coldness. The party was over. I didn't understand or acknowledge the many red flags. I was his adamant defender. I believed he couldn't help his actions because of his history. He blamed everyone and took no accountability, but I believed I could help him heal if he just let me.

After his release, we lived together. As is typical with the pattern of abuse, the violence intensified. A woman will leave and return to an abusive relationship on average seven times. For me, the first few times I returned were out of "love" and the hope that things would change. Later, I returned because of fear. I vividly remember the Christmas gift my big sister gave me, the book: *Women Who Love Too Much*. Reading that book was a turning point. I finally realized that I had to love myself *more* if I wanted to live.

Attempting to leave a violent relationship is a dangerous time. After failed escapes, my very last attempt was a plea for reason and rationale. I asked for understanding. I was, in effect, begging his permission to leave him! I didn't know what else to do. To my surprise and relief, he agreed! *Really? Oh my God, thank you!* I thought. "Can we just have one last night out?" he asked. "Let me take you out to dinner to say good-bye." "Well, okay," I answered, thinking *We will be in public.*

That seems safe enough. I should've known he had no intention of just "setting me free." After dinner, we sat in my car together, and I was ready for him to leave. I could hardly believe this was actually happening! I felt nervous, yet calmly guarded. He finally realized I indeed was going to say good-bye and drive off for good. This was the first time I broke our usual pattern of "I forgive you. We can try again." With his realization came a swift blow to my head with his fist. In that panicked moment, I threw the car into gear and drove off with him sitting next to me! Just ahead I saw a cop car parked at the Tasty Freeze. *Thank you, God!* I sped up to it.

What happened next happened so fast that I only remember a few segments: The officer's car pulled up next to my window, and he asked me if everything was okay. My words told him *yes*, but I hoped he could tell that my eyes were saying *no*. With a helpful fight or flight response, I quickly grabbed my keys and made a mad dash out of the car, running and hiding behind the officer for protection. The officer attempted to handcuff him, but he resisted. I didn't wait for a conclusion. I got back in my car and sped off, driving right over the concrete meridian! My heart was racing, and I felt a mix of fear and relief. I immediately went to my friend's house to call the police station to make sure I was safe and that he was in jail, naively assuming he would be. I learned that he wasn't. This was before the Domestic Violence Act, which allows an officer to make an arrest without the victim having to press charges. Knowing he was not in jail, I couldn't stay at my friend's house, and I certainly did not want to worry my parents. I went to my boss's house, where I knew he would never think to find me.

It took time for me to recover from that six-year relationship. The physical bruises faded, but the emotional bruises lingered. However, what goes up must come down. Right and wrong, black and white, hot and cold—there is an opposite to *everything*, and this also holds true for emotions. Without experiencing sadness, we could not know happiness. Without challenge, we cannot grow, and without fear, we cannot know courage. It was that relationship that inspired me to pursue psychology and become the therapist I am today. I wanted to help young women caught in the domestic violence trap. It was also that relationship that led me to the beautiful man I have today. When I finally made it out for good, I made a key decision to never settle for less in a relationship again and to do what I could to help others. For that I am grateful.

If you or someone you know is in a domestic violence situation, there is hope and help. Please call the National Domestic Violence Hotline at 1(800) 799-7233.

The "not enough" disease inevitably attacks us all at some point. Our true selves—our authentic selves—are still there living inside us, but sometimes they are hidden because of fear. My true *self* is and always has been that *go-go-go!* girl. Throughout life, I always wanted to go for the gusto! But fear stopped me every time. With every opportunity, with every life decision, I feared what others would think. I feared making mistakes, I feared failure, and as an adult I learned that I also feared success. Fear and anxiety tricked me to believe that I wasn't enough and that I couldn't have, be, or do all that I desired. Luckily, I was also cursed (or blessed?) with a very strong fear of regret. We can learn to use our fear as fuel. Although I won't say that the fear of regret is a high *quality* gasoline, I have—and sometimes still do—choose that grade at the pump.

I never wanted to live with regret in any area of my life—relationships, career, or otherwise. I didn't *want* to settle, but that's exactly what I did. Instead of pursing my dream of becoming a therapist, I made it my hobby to be a client. When asked what I wanted from counseling, I said, "I want to do what *you* do! *But I'm not capable.*" Fortunately, the fear of regret turned the "not enough" disease into *dis*-ease. At some point in every single job, I would begin to feel a sense of unease, a low-grade discomfort. Thank God for those moments of slight pain. Pain is a signal to help you know that something is off. For me, it was my cue to change course. One day I found myself standing at another of those proverbial doors. This time it was literally the entrance door of my factory job. I was just about to go in for my shift, and I felt a sense of "dis-ease" stronger than ever. Before going in, I stood at that door for a moment and did something I had never done before and would never do again. I turned around and left! Filled with guilt, I made a mad rush home to call in sick and give my notice. (There were no cell phones back then!) I felt guilty *and* free!

Some of my job choices had been fun, and I could have easily stayed with them. I love music and photography, so I worked developing film in a music store. When I wasn't busy developing film, I could crank the tunes and dance around to INXS while dusting the stereo equipment! I loved it, but I longed for a career. I wanted so badly to attend school for *something*, so I decided to become a hairstylist. Staying true to my *go-go-go!* nature, I envisioned being a stylist to the stars—*rock* stars, that is! Free from my abusive relationship, I returned to my free and independent spirit. I returned to the "*don't settle, big dreamer* me." And if I couldn't have Big Dream A, then Big Dream B would do. So, off to the big city of Syracuse I went. I had an amazing time. I graduated and immediately found work. I was free and independent. I bought my dream car, a brand new 1988 Mustang! I had my very own apartment on the lake. Life was good.

As time went on, though, I decided that I was more gifted at *talking* with my clients than I was cutting their hair. I was having fun, and I probably would have stayed, but the dis-ease kicked in again. You know, when you ignore symptoms they tend to intensify until you have no choice but to take action. One day while standing at my stylist chair enjoying my time with my client, I had an unexpected out-of-the-blue panic attack—a *sign*? I attributed it to coffee and quit caffeine cold turkey. Inevitably, I quit the beauty biz as well.

Temporary Detour: Exit career dreams, enter man of my dreams

I believe that when you absolutely know what you want, why you want it, and you get out of your own way to allow it, the universe delivers quickly. I believe that is exactly how I found Craig.

I saw him for the first time at a crossroad. Yes, it was literally a crossroad just before dawn, where I had stopped at a four-way traffic light. I was in the right lane, he the left. *Who is that?* I wondered. I found out just a few days later on my twenty-fifth birthday, where I met him for the first time at a hometown bar. After that night we were inseparable. We had both recently sworn off relationships, so it made it safe for us to just "be." It was effortless to stay awake until 5 a.m. talking, telling our stories, and learning everything to know about each other. It was so easy, and within two weeks we were in love and planning our "forever." He was my marine, and once again I was safe and sound.

We quickly built a life together and bought a piece of property in the middle of nowhere with just a farmer's path and no electrical access. But it had a pond, and we had a vision! Our vision started as a stick-drawing on a napkin and manifested into the reality we live today. Over time we planted over a thousand trees, developed a functional driveway, and brought in electricity. The blizzard of 1993 forced us to invest in a snowplow and to trade in the Mustang for a Bronco. We parked our mobile home on our property and saved our pennies to build our dream home.

Anxiety would visit periodically during the early years of our relationship, but I never understood why. Things were going so well! But, you see, sometimes old fears have a way of hanging around when there is nothing to be afraid of, even when things are going really well. Old fears park themselves in our unconscious and live within us on a cellular level. That unconsciously-held core belief that I wasn't enough—combined with my childhood learning that it wasn't okay for me to shine—triggered anxiety at the most important time of my adult life. One source of anxiety was the thought of walking down the aisle on my wedding day. *What if I have a panic attack right there in front of everyone? What if I pass out? Now* I see what that *really* meant: *Who are you to have such a great life? A great man, a beautiful wedding—who are you to shine.*

Honeymoon plans were also affected. I hadn't always been afraid of travel; in fact, I had loved it. But for a while after my first panic attack, I was afraid of traveling long distances and afraid of boat rides, both of which were necessary to get us to where we wanted to go—Nova Scotia. I wanted a dream wedding, and I was determined to figure it all out. So, I did what I loved doing; I went to therapy with the hope of overcoming these fears. Needless to say, my old therapy hobby didn't do the trick, but I cured my fear of walking down the aisle by deciding to have both my mom *and* dad beside me. That and a nip of champagne in the Rolls on my way to the church gave me the courage I didn't think I had. Let me just say that I do *not* recommend a nip of alcohol to ease wedding jitters, but both parents down the aisle was definitely a hit and I would do that again—anxiety or no anxiety.

As far as the honeymoon? Well, unfortunately, I went to my old standby safety measure, avoidance. We traded our honeymoon dream for a close-to-home weekend trip to Niagara Falls. Less travel and less time away from home eased my anxiety some, but still I remember feeling low-grade nausea most of the time. I thought I was coming down with the flu. I often thought I was coming down with the flu, but now I know that that is just one of the common symptoms of anxiety. Back then I was never without my emergency collection of Advil, a thermometer, and Pepto-Bismol.

It's important to understand that our fear about our anxiety symptoms (the fear of the fear) is *never* as big as we think it is. We tend to imagine the worst-case scenario in our minds, and our bodies naturally respond to that movie we create in our heads. The reality, though, was nothing like I had imagined. Did I feel nervous? Yes. Did I pass out? No! And even if I had, even if the worst-case scenario had come true, I would have lived; I would have survived the embarrassment. During that time and so many others, I wasted so much precious time and missed savoring so many memorable moments all due to worry. Worrying about something that never even happened was stolen time that could have been spent enjoying life to the fullest.

As time was pressing on, I set my sights back to a career. My deep love for animals led me to my next attempt at career fulfillment.

I grew up with every animal one can think of—from cats and dogs to mice and guinea pigs to raccoons and skunks. I grew up watching my mom tend to abandoned or injured wildlife. I especially remember the bottle-fed raccoons and the oven-hatched robins that she carefully hand-fed worms to. I remember once having sat for what seemed like hours next to a truck that a dog was scared to come out from under. I sat there calmly until she felt safe to come out. I was easing animals' anxieties before ever helping myself or my human clients! In 1990, a trip to Watkin's Glen Farm Sanctuary, a safe haven for abused farm animals, unexpectedly woke us up from the matrix that we and most people live in. We chose to take the "red pill" and saw the undeniable reality of the suffering animals endure in the name of food. We made the connection and became vegetarians. By 1993 I had my dream job as a veterinary receptionist. I loved it, but once again felt the familiar tug of dis-ease and the pull toward higher education dreams.

Dreams, now of the nocturnal type, started to call. Throughout my twenties, I periodically had dreams of walking down my high school halls crying because I missed it so much. At age twenty-nine, I was having these dreams almost nightly. Nagging dreams! I could not ignore the message coming in loud and clear as I approached the big 3-0 birthday: *it's time to make a decision; now or never.*

Turning thirty, I chose *now*. I didn't know *how* I was going to get around my fear of public speaking, but I had to figure it out. Being a talented and skilled avoider, I knew I would. *I won't tell anyone I'm going*, I thought. *That way if I fail, I can spare the embarrassment and humiliation. Baby steps. I'll start with a free continuing education course to see if I can even sit in a classroom without running out screaming. I will sit by the door, just in case.*

And that is what I did. In 1994, the year I turned thirty, I finally began my pursuit of happiness and enrolled at Finger Lakes Community College.

During college, I was not *only* tested on paper. Yes, I was passionately learning and excelling academically beyond my wildest expectations—finally dispelling the "not smart enough" lie. But, interestingly, the bigger I grew, so did the anxiety. *Warning, warning! Shine meter is over capacity!* The original public speaking fear unexpectedly metastasized into a debilitating panic disorder with agoraphobia. I had out-of-the blue feelings of irrational fear followed by feelings of shame, disappointment, and sadness for not having the ability to control it. Once again, life became very difficult, and I lost the freedoms we tend to take for granted. Once again, daily tasks like driving, riding, and errands were challenged. Things I had always enjoyed—like traveling, dancing, and shopping—were out of the question. College was now something I feared. I literally could not walk across the stage and accept any of my college diplomas. For my first college graduation, I practiced walking back and forth on the stage while no one was there, but that didn't work so I stayed home. For the next degree—at Nazareth College—I again bought my cap and gown but could only watch from the audience as my classmates walked the stage. I remember feeling embarrassed and disappointed in myself because my husband, parents, and sister were all there to see me graduate. I wasn't leaving campus without at least one picture of me in my cap and gown. By the time I graduated from Syracuse University, I didn't even consider walking the stage, because the venue was just too big. My proudest moments turned to shame and sadness. Fearing the fear made my world shrink smaller and smaller.

During my undergrad years I tried therapy, but the therapist suggested I see a doctor for a prescription. *Not* what I was looking for. I wanted *tools*, someone to tell me what to *do*! But, I obliged, since it appeared to be my only option, and after a brief consult with an MD, I was given a script for Prozac. Of course, I didn't take it, because medication was just another fear. Fortunately, my major was psychology. I was learning about different theoretical approaches. That is when I discovered cognitive therapy, and that changed everything for me! With cognitive therapy I learned that my thoughts were triggering my panic symptoms. I learned how to track, test, challenge, and change my thoughts. Years later, I heard Wayne Dyer say: "Change your thoughts and you change your world." That is the truth! Cognitive therapy was so successful for me that I vowed to one day specialize in it and become a certified cognitive therapist— which I did years later in 2010.

No longer plagued with active panic symptoms, I finally fulfilled my dream of becoming a mental health therapist. For years I had "end goal" thinking, but I have learned that there is no final goal, no end destination. Rather, true fulfillment is a journey filled with achievements along the way, new dreams, goals, and constant growth. I had the next phase all figured out: gain experience, work for an agency for a few years and— for the next big dream—open my own private practice. All was well; there was no more dis-ease. For awhile anyway …

Then I hit forty.

I think if I had turned forty during quiet weather, I would have embraced the beginning of the decade with grace and ease. But the decade of my fortieth year began quite stormy, and it was dark for a while. My sister developed brain cancer. My father's chronic health issues worsened. Of course, my driving anxiety returned. Driving back and forth to the hospital, my hands would be wet on the wheel with every big rig in front of me, behind me, or beside me. But I was quickly able to quell that fear. You see, all her life my sister panicked at the thought of needles, yet she was forced to muster up all her courage every day during her cancer treatments. While driving, all I had to do was proclaim: "This is absolutely nothing! Look at all Ann has to endure. Peg, you can fucking drive!" Two of the most loving, kind, and generous spirits I have ever known, left their physical bodies: Ann at age fifty—and my dad sixteen months later at age seventy-seven.

A year after Dad died, my marriage encountered a crisis. I won't get into the details here, but that story just might be the next book. I don't believe I would be able to help couples the way I do if not for that experience. It shook us both to our core, but we came back from it transformed for the better. Just as we began our healing journey, we unexpectedly lost our two fur kids one month apart from each other. Cancer showed up again for Mack, and Maggie was killed in our yard by a trespasser on a four-wheeler. If you know us, you know our pets are not just pets; they are our children.

The passing of my sister, my father, our marital crisis, and the deaths of our fur children at the starting gate of turning forty shocked my system. However, shocks to the system can wake you up. "In all pain is a warning or a lesson," I heard someone say, and *yes*, that is the truth. The fear of regret had always been strong in me, but these life challenges just put me in overdrive! I wanted more than ever to live with purpose and intention. I wanted to love more, give more, be more, and live more! My initial mistake was allowing the fear to drive me *too* much. This resulted in never-before-experienced health anxiety. I had never thought about my health much at all prior to this. Remember, I was the one who smoked cigarettes and rationalized that I didn't smoke that much and that I didn't want to live to be one hundred anyway! I finally quit smoking, but interestingly, it had nothing to do with *trying* to quit; instead, it was my dear friend, Kim, who is also my hairdresser. While doing my hair, she said: "You know, Peg, I am so surprised you smoke. It really doesn't fit with how I see you." That was it! I did not smoke a day after that! No patches, no white-knuckle motivation needed! That is not who I *am*, and she was right. Who I *am* is an optimist, a longtime exerciser, a vegetarian. It was weird for her to see me smoke, because she saw *me* through the smoke. I smoked, true, but I am not "a smoker!" That was just a label, just a story. The stories we tell ourselves—and you will see there are many—are just beliefs, and beliefs aren't always truth.

Between my sister's cancer history and my father's type 1 diabetes and rheumatoid arthritis, I needed reassurance. Reassurance for myself, and reassurance that the rest of my loved ones left in my life were not going anywhere soon. After seeing what they went through, fear once again drove me to take action, but *this* time it was positive, *preventive* action. I used to believe with 100 percent certainty that aging meant suffering—feeling sick, tired, and in pain. I used to believe that if you were going to get sick that meant unfortunate genes. I now know we have more control over the aging process and the condition of our health and bodies. Yes, of course genes matter, but now I take control of what I can control, and I let go of that which is out of my control.

Whereas my early forties was a time of pain, the later forties was a time of growth and action. I spent the rest of my forties learning and growing my knowledge base for my health, my practice, and my personal life. During those years I thought I was eating a healthy vegetarian diet, but what I learned was that I was a junk food vegetarian. I was also learning so much about the food-mood connection: how what we eat can affect not only our physical health but also our emotional health. I wanted to share what I was learning with my clients. I knew I could help them so much more with their anxiety challenges, but I was professionally limited for lack of credentials in this area. I graduated from the Institute of Integrative Nutrition and added holistic health coach to my credentials for exactly this reason. And to have specialized knowledge in plant-based nutrition, I am currently studying at the Vegetarian Health Institute. I am now armed with information that I wish I had had long before my dad and my sister became ill. I cannot do anything for them now, but I can take control of my own health. I can care for my still-living loved ones in a way I didn't know how to then and I can share this knowledge with others.

It was also in my later forties that I became a certified cognitive therapist, strategic interventionist and nlp practitioner. Learning strategic intervention was a blessing that came into my life just in time to help transform my own marriage, and it is now my go-to for helping other couples. No more travel anxiety! I flew from New York to California to study with master therapist Cloe Madanes, and while there, I unexpectedly met my favorite spiritual teacher, Wayne Dyer. One night when I was alone in my hotel room it hit me just how much anxiety I had overcome. I can't believe I am *here* doing *this!* During those years, my husband and I brought our marriage to new heights, and we adopted a new fur family. Later we built a home for my mom so she could be safe and sound. I tell you this because life inevitably brings pain, but it also brings blessings. The key is not to *live* in the pain. Don't deny it, don't put a flower on a piece of dog poop. Shit is shit! But you can use that crap for fertilizer. That is the truth!

Now it is more than twenty years later. I am in my fiftieth decade at the time of this writing. I am happy to tell you that I am free from Anxiety State Prison! I am grateful beyond measure that I finally found the tools I was looking for—tools that have helped me condition my mind, body, and spirit. Through the years, I gathered my personal learnings and added them into a holistic toolbox, the same toolbox I continue to use and now give to my clients. The most important realization for me was that the keys to unlock the cell door were within me the whole time! I *now* see that anxiety was and still is a gift! It's an evolutionary, instinctual gift given *for me*, alerting me to danger or to remind me to prepare for life's stages and responsibilities. It's also a personal gift, because I truly believe I would not be in this position I am in today—helping many anxiety sufferers overcome their fears—if not for all I had experienced.

That all said, I cannot end my story without telling you about a very magical moment. Yes, what goes around comes around. In 2011, I was asked to speak to a class of fifth graders about anxiety. My first opportunity to speak, and it had to be with children, standing between their desks just like where I started my anxiety story. Go figure! There are no coincidences, my friends! There was still a part of me that was scared, a five-year-old who was traumatized. But there was also a part of me that knew no fear. That was an interesting experience—to feel both at once! My personal coach was an amazing support who helped me get in tip-top emotional fitness. Only allowing myself to create and see a movie of success in my mind, I planned a celebration lunch with my hubby for immediately after. On the drive to the school, I anchored myself to KC and the Sunshine Band's "Keep It Coming Love," the first song I heard when I turned on the radio. It continues to be my confidence anchor! So there I was speaking to a class of middle schoolers, with their teachers watching; I was feeling so grateful, excited, and proud. What if there was a child struggling just like I did? What if I can make a difference for them now? I purposefully planned for the talk to happen on my birthday, and I officially coined that forty-seventh year my "rebirth" day! The day I was done with fear!

So you see, anxiety is a necessary emotion, but it's not meant to be a prison sentence. I would have died in my soul, though, had I not taken heed to those recurring dreams warning me to *get out!* Now there's a *real* horror flick! Do I still experience anxiety? Absolutely! In fact, awhile ago while driving to the airport, old familiar feelings of panic returned in full force. *What is going on?* I wondered. I hadn't experienced driving anxiety in years! I was freaking out on the thruway and called a friend for support. I realized it was because I needed to decide on a new and unknown course, a path that would once again push me into new growth and opportunities. It had been quite some time since I had stretched so far outside my comfort zone. Anxiety was showing up as it did years ago to keep me safe and sound, to make sure I kept my shine meter in check. But there was no danger, nothing to keep me safe from. It was just a growth spurt with some added growing pains. Now, the question is, do I decide to dim my light and play small, or live with freedom? By getting on the plane I realized I had already decided. I smiled to myself: "*go-go-go girl*, it's time to show-and-tell!"

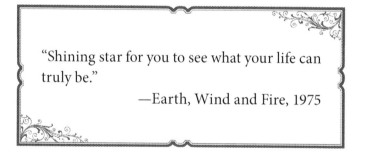

"Shining star for you to see what your life can truly be."

—Earth, Wind and Fire, 1975

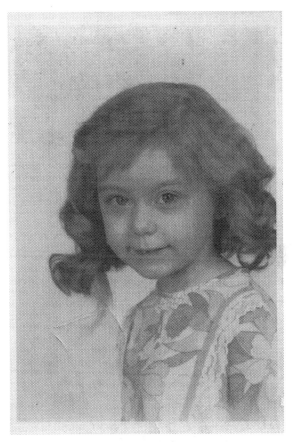

Kindergarten; let the fears begin!

My deep love for animals began early. In the 1970s we
did not think twice about sleeping with racoons!

My Marine then and now 1989 and present

The day Craig and I became a vegetarians. Farm
Sanctuary Watkins Glen, NY 1990

Walking down the isle with a little help form my parents! 1992

I attended my Nazareth College graduation ceremony, but
could only watch from the audience. A bitter sweet day.

My dad and sister when they were both sick. New found purpose
to help others, my loved ones and myself to better health.

Mom enjoying a green smoothie. In her 80th decade and loving life!

Fear To Freedom! My first firewalk! I have since
hosted a firewalk for my clients! They loved it!

A magic moment to run into one of my favorite
spiritual teachers Wayne Dyer

Dedicated to Health AND Happiness!

Growing and expanding with my dream. Breaking
ground for my second office location!

Note from Peg:

Thank you for joining me on my personal journey of fear to freedom. I hope you now realize you are not alone and that there is hope. Truth be told, while writing my story I felt a bit vulnerable. *Who am I to write a book,* I wondered. *What will others think? Is it good enough? Am I good enough?* Yes, the old fears show up as I am about to push once again outside my comfort zone by allowing others to see *me.* And as I write this right now today—the day I planned to hand the first draft to Balboa publishing—I awoke this morning (August 31, 2015) to hear of Wayne Dyer's passing. He was one of my favorite spiritual teachers, and I am reminded not to let the music die within me—that what others think is none of my business. This message was on his daily calendar today on my desk:

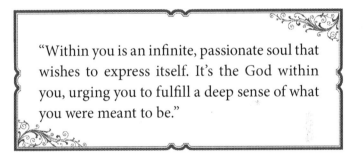

"Within you is an infinite, passionate soul that wishes to express itself. It's the God within you, urging you to fulfill a deep sense of what you were meant to be."

Thank you, Wayne. I am not letting the music die in me—not today, not ever. And I will do my best to share that truth with others, too.

Vulnerability is fear, and facing fear leads to courage. I encourage you to write your story. It can lead to insights and self-awareness that you had no idea existed. Only in writing my story did I realize that this book isn't really even about overcoming anxiety. It was never about anxiety, stress, or panic attacks at all! It was, is, and always will be about *freedom.* My anxiety showed up when my freedom to shine—to be authentically me—was threatened by someone or by my own imagined fears. This book is really about claiming your right to be authentically you—no apologies! I will give you the tools. I will give you the strategies, but it is *you* who already possess all you need. You are the keys. *This* is what I want you to take away most from my story and this book.

Rise and shine,
Peg

I cannot wait to coach you and support you on your way to leaving your prison once and for all and to see you on the other side of that prison gate. So let's get started by identifying *your* story of where you are now and even better, where you want to be …

- Complete: Point A: Life on the Inside; Your "Mug Shot" Assessment
- Complete: Point B: Life on the Outside! Your Freedom Awaits!

POINT A: LIFE ON THE INSIDE; "MUG SHOT" ASSESSMENT

All prisoners have a mug shot, right? Consider this yours. This is your Point A, where you are now. This is about everything you are currently struggling with. You will use this same tool to assess your midpoint and end results, so I suggest you print out three copies before you write on the original. Filling out this assessment may or may not create more feelings of anxiety in you. This is normal, and don't be afraid. It's only because as you are filling out the form, you are focusing on your problem. If you are focused on your problem, it's natural for you to *feel* that problem. Feel free to share this assessment with your primary care doctor or other health professionals. Remember, it is very important to rule out medical causes first, and this assessment tool can be incorporated into your existing care plan.

My advice: be honest! You may not like some of your answers, and you may be tempted to soften them, but the truth shall set you free! Remember, you will be reassessing again at midpoint and again at the end, and you will want to celebrate your progress! Use this worksheet to answer the following questions.

Body

In this category the focus is on identifying physiological sensations that may occur during anxiety, the nourishment you're giving your body, your physical activity level, and the quality of sleep and relaxation your body is getting.

Panic/Anxiety Inventory
Below is a list of some common physiological sensations that occur during an anxiety or panic state. Please check all that apply during an anxious time.

_____ Shakiness
_____ Diarrhea
_____ Difficulty breathing or shortness of breath
_____ Nausea
_____ Hands trembling
_____ Abdominal distress/pain
_____ Rapid or pounding heart
_____ Muscle tension
_____ Numbness/tingling
_____ Headaches
_____ Hot flashes
_____ Sweating
_____ Unsteadiness or dizziness
_____ Choking feeling
_____ Other: _____

On average, how many times do you experience panic attacks in a week? _____ Last week?_____

How long do they last, generally?_____

How much do they bother you? Circle one:

Mildly   Moderately   Severely

Does anxiety cause you to avoid certain events or situations? Have you passed up opportunities because of it? If so, please list and explain.

Are you experiencing feelings of sadness, depression, or hopelessness?

If so, how would you rate the intensity of these feelings on a scale of 0–10, where

0=none and 10=the most severe unsafe/suicidal thoughts?

> ***If you are experiencing intense feelings of depression and are feeling unsafe with yourself or having intentional thoughts of suicide, please get help now by calling 911, who will assist in connecting you with your local lifeline or mental health emergency services.***

How is your energy level on an average day? Circle one.

Great	I have energy throughout the day without caffeine.
Good	A little slow in the morning and midafternoon, but I don't need caffeine.
Fair	I usually need a morning and midafternoon caffeine fix.
Poor	I live on caffeine and energy drinks to function.

Food and Substances

Caffeine: What and how much? Besides coffee, don't forget to include unexpected or often forgotten sources, like chocolate, tea, medications, energy drinks, and energy shots.

Alcohol: How many alcoholic beverages do you consume in a day/ week, on average?

Medication: Are you taking any psychotropic meds for anxiety or depression? Please list type, dose, and start date.

Do not change or discontinue any medication regimen without consulting your health care professional.

Daily Meals

Please write out your typical daily meal regimen in detail. Write "none" if applicable.

Breakfast:

Midmorning snack:

Lunch:

Midafternoon snack:

Dinner:

Evening snack:

Supplements:

Herbal remedies:

How much plain water (lemon added okay) do you consume in a day?

Do you binge eat?

How many days of the week do you eat fast food?

How often do you consume foods high in sugar and/or preservatives?

    Circle: Daily   Weekly   Rarely

Have you ever been diagnosed with or do you have symptoms of IBS (irritable bowel syndrome)? (This is common with chronic anxiety sufferers.)

Sleep

    Total hours per night, on average:

      Bedtime: Waking time:

Trouble falling asleep? Y   N   Sometimes # Nights per week_____

Trouble staying asleep? Y   N   Sometimes # Nights per week_____

Nightmares?   Y   N   Sometimes # Nights per week_____
Overall quality of sleep: Good   Fair   Poor

Movement

    Do you participate in any form of physical exercise?

    How often? _____days out of seven, for _____minutes a day.

Mind-set

In this category, the focus is on thoughts, perceptions, and beliefs. Please rate each statement 0–10, with 0 being the least true of you and 10 being absolutely true of you. Answer with your first gut-level response:

____ I tend to be a worrier.

____ I tend to take things personally; I'm pretty sensitive.

____ What if! What if! What if!

____ I have to admit, I'm a pretty negative thinker.

____ I've always been an anxious person.

____I've always been a shy person.

____I worry what others think of me.

____I often think I don't measure up; I'm not good enough or smart enough.

____ I imagine the worst-case scenario in many situations.

____I am a perfectionist.

____I am a people pleaser.

____Feeling certain, having a routine, and knowing the plan all sound really good.

____I get bored easily.

____I'm easily stressed over everyday common life challenges (hectic days, etc.).

____It's important to be successful in whatever I do.

____It's easy for me to love and trust people.

In the next exercise, think about what you want from life. If you are not where you want to be in your life right now, what do you think prevents you from having the life you want? Check all that apply:

____ Panic or anxiety challenge

____ Low self-confidence

____ Fear of change

____Fear of success

____ Fear of failure

____Fear of rejection

____Fear of disappointing others

____ Lack of time

____ Lack of motivation

____Disorganization

____Feeling overwhelmed

____Other people

____Depression

____Fear of disapproval

____ Situations beyond my control

____Relationship concerns

____Money issues

____Other:

Spirit

Here you are going to look at how you feed your spirit: the quality of your relationships, the stability of your environment, personal growth, and contribution. For now just reflect on your current situations.

Do you have a spiritual or religious belief? _____ If so, are you happy with the amount of time you commit to it?

Are you in an intimate relationship?

If so, how satisfied are you in the relationship? Please rate 0–10, with 0 meaning "I'm out of here!" and 10 meaning "I am happy and fulfilled!"

Domestic violence: Do you feel safe emotionally and physically in this relationship?

Is your partner understanding and supportive when it comes to your anxiety challenges?

What about other relationships? Do you have a support network of family and friends?

Do you work inside or outside the home? If so, please rate job satisfaction 0–10, with 0 meaning "I need out!" and 10 meaning "I couldn't be happier!"

Do you have interests or hobbies outside of work?

Do you volunteer?

If retired, how has your life changed for the better or worse?

Is there financial stress, health-related stress, or any extraordinary stressor in your life right now? If so, what?

Do you have children?

Do you have pets?

Do you feel fulfilled? If not, then what do you believe is missing? What do you think you need to feel fulfilled?

POINT B: LIFE ON THE OUTSIDE; YOUR FREEDOM AWAITS!

Have you ever thought about what you would do if only you were not challenged by excessive anxiety, panic, frustration, procrastination, or low confidence? This will take some time and thought, but *do not* skip this step! Whereas point A is your "before pic," this is your Point B, or your "after pic." These are the results you want to achieve and why you want to achieve them. This is your life outside of Anxiety Prison. I cannot stress enough how important this step is! Without this step you will not get the results you seek, because not knowing what you want and why you want it will make you quit when it gets uncomfortable; you will put this program on the shelf to collect dust, and create a story about why it didn't work for you. I am not going to let you do that! It's time to …

Identify Your Freedom!

What **exactly do I want?** Give yourself this gift. Grab a cup of chamomile tea, get your journal, and take some time now to write about what it is you want. When was the last time someone asked you, or when was the last time you asked yourself: *What do I really want for my life? What would I do, what would I be, what would I accomplish if this anxiety challenge was gone. If I had all the courage I needed, if fear was not a factor, what would be different? How would I feel differently? How would I behave differently? What opportunities would I take or seek out? What does freedom from anxiety look like for me?* I can't tell you how many people I have talked with who tell me what they want to be, do, or have—and then they immediately shift to all the reasons why they can't have them. And here's the thing—just like my experience, they think their dreams are too big! But, the truth is their desires aren't extraordinary! It's just their fear talking. What do *your* fears keep you from? Do you dream of having a wonderful relationship full of passion and love? Do you dream of owning your own home? Do you dream of starting a business offering something you love? Do you dream of writing a book? Do you want to go back to school? These are just some of the things I often hear people would love to do "if they only could." Take some time to write about what you want. It's your turn. Dare to dream!

What do I want? If anxiety was not a challenge I would ...

_____

_____

_____

_____

_____

_____

_____

_____

_____

_____

_____

_____

Why do I want it? Now that you know *what* you want, even more important is to know *why* you want it. You have committed to doing the work in this book. Why? Why are you putting in the effort? What are you doing this all for? Getting really clear on this will get you through the most challenging times. This is true for any dream, goal, or desire. Moving away from pain will motivate you to do this work, but it will only work in the short-term. With a big enough *why* you will find a way, because this will move you continuously forward. So ask yourself, *Why do I want what I want? What will it mean for me? What will it mean for those I love? What could it mean for others? How could I make a difference to the world if I fulfilled my dreams? How does this relate to my purpose?*

Why do I want that? Having or accomplishing all that I want would mean …

_____

_____

_____

_____

_____

_____

_____

_____

_____

_____

_____.

You know that you have completed this part of the exercise in the most beneficial way when you can say: "That's it! This anxiety problem has to go *now*!"

Here is an example of how one client completed both parts of this exercise for herself. Notice how clear and specific her wants are and how her *why* has the emotional charge necessary.

What do I want? If anxiety was not a challenge, I would …

If anxiety was not a challenge, I would go for my biggest goal in my life: return to school to become a registered nurse. I would travel and eventually become a traveling RN! I would attract a loving, committed relationship that I have as yet only been wishing for. I would find a way to become completely financially independent. After pursuing my first passion, nursing, later in life I would become a hairstylist and makeup artist part-time.

Why do I want that?

Accomplishing that would mean I would become more self-fulfilled and happy! I would have so much confidence! I would be able to help people out of the goodness of my heart, no matter what. With anxiety out of the way, I could do that! Dad has been such an inspiration for beating cancer time and time again, and my mother works hard with her many health issues present. If I was a nurse, I could contribute so much for them. Not to mention all the people who will need me and who I will serve as a nurse. Not just the patients, but their loved ones too! I would have opportunities to make new friends and be a friend—friends that I might not ever meet if I don't pursue my dreams. *And* if I was debt-free, I would be able to repay my parents for all that they have done for me and help them for what they are going through. As for fulfilling my artistic goals in life, I will be free to express my creative side! I had many opportunities working with my friends that are hairstylists. I will be able to help others feel beautiful inside (as a nurse) and out! And with anxiety out of my way, I just might realize that I have the greatest qualities to offer someone, and settling for something that is less than what I deserve won't be happening. All in all, making a difference in someone's life, now and in the future, will be truly amazing!

Now that you specifically know what you want and realize there is no option but to have it, how are you going to get out of your own way to get it? There are three keys that—when used together—will unlock the door to your anxiety prison and set you free for life. I am sharing them in the order in which I received them for myself. I didn't obtain them all at once. I wish I had, because I would have gained the long-term benefits sooner. I am grateful I have all the keys now and that I can share them with you all at once!

PART II

THE THREE KEYS
TO FREEDOM

KEY #1  FREEDOM FOR YOUR MIND

False Arrest! I've been Conned!

> "Of all the liars in the world, sometimes the worst are your own fears."
>
> —Rudyard Kipling

F.E.A.R. What is fear, really? I love the analogy I saw quite a few years back that said *fear* is *false* *evidence* *appearing* *real*. This is so true, but in order to buy this you have to become *aware* of a few things first.

The first key unlocks freedom for your mind; the first key is awareness. These are the very first things I needed to know and the first thing I share with you now. It's awareness of what anxiety is and what it is not—and awareness of the thought-mood connection. For me, knowing this alone resulted in immediate relief.

Be Aware: Anxiety is a con! It tricks us into believing that we could literally die, go crazy, or have a heart attack. I do not say this to minimize your experience; I know that what you are experiencing is at the very least significantly uncomfortable and at its worst, imprisoning—hence, the metaphor for this book. But I want you to understand that what you are experiencing, although highly distressing, is not dangerous, life-threatening, or life-sentencing.

Fear is a necessary response to *real* danger. Anxiety is an emotion and is actually helpful to prompt us to prepare for something we are probably not prepared for. Have you prepared for that meeting? Have you studied for that test? But anxiety, the *con artist,* tries to convince us that it's so much more. That happens when anxiety is triggered by *perceived* imminent danger. Anxiety shows up with *fearful thoughts* of future events or *fearful thoughts* of past events. *Panic* is the physiological reaction we have in response to fear and anxiety. *Stress* is associated with our day-to-day life frustrations. There is definitely overlap between stress, fear, and anxiety, and they are often words used interchangeably. However, when we are stressed, we know what we are stressed about; with panic or anxiety, we commonly don't know or don't understand what we are fearful about. That unknowing can create debilitating fear, and on we go with the cycle.

With true imminent danger comes the fight-flight-freeze response. (Remember me jumping out of my car to get away from danger?) This is a necessary survival function for nonhuman animals and for us. As cave people, we needed it to survive possible attacks from saber-toothed tigers. We had three choices: fight the tiger, flee the tiger, or freeze and hope the tiger didn't see us! We still need that survival instinct these days, but it's less likely going to be a threat from a tiger, unless you're picking on one in captivity—so please don't do that! Today it might mean an attack from a mugger or a robber. The challenge, however, is when this amazing and necessary survival instinct fires off when there is no actual danger present. It's like the fire alarm going off when there is no fire. When you are sound asleep and you are awakened by the fire alarm, or when you are sound asleep and awakened by an extremely upsetting nightmare, it makes sense if you experience one or more of the following physiological sensations:

- palpitations, pounding heart, or accelerated heart rate
- sweating

- trembling or shaking
- sensations of shortness of breath or smothering
- a feeling of choking
- chest pain or discomfort
- nausea or abdominal distress
- feeling dizzy, unsteady, lightheaded, or faint
- feelings of unreality or being detached from oneself
- numbness or tingling sensations
- chills or hot flashes

This is a list of symptoms common to a panic attack, and it's also what we may experience when we're faced with real danger. Getting back to the fire alarm or bad dream, as soon as you look around and realize there is no fire or realize it was a dream, what happens? Do the physiological sensations start to dissipate? Yes. Why? Because you now realize it was a false alarm or a nightmare; you realize there is no *real* danger. You give it a different meaning, and you start to focus on going back to sleep, knowing you are safe.

Your body does not know the difference between real danger and perceived danger. It is the thoughts you are thinking that differentiate them.

Of course, it's frightening to have these responses (symptoms) in our bodies for no apparent reason. Because there is no danger present, we can't make sense of our body's response. We naturally believe that there must be something wrong, so the pattern begins:

Mild bodily sensations occur.

Thoughts begin: *Oh no, here it comes.*

Mental pictures: You see yourself losing control.

Body sensations now increase *because you just scared yourself* with your thought and mental picture.

Scarier thoughts occur: *Oh my gosh, this means I really am …* [fill in your fear with the list below or add your own]!

Body sensations increase again, leading to a full-blown fear response or panic reaction.

Your first panic attack may have come unexpectedly, out of the blue, *or* in response to a situation. Either way, the intensity of the body sensations causes us to now "fear the fear," meaning we don't understand what happened; we become afraid of the symptoms and do our best to prevent them from happening again. Unless the pattern is broken, we might end up in a maximum-security prison, meaning that the longer this pattern continues, the more it limits our freedom.

Here is how one client described it:

"I had no idea what was happening when I had my first panic attack. It came unexpectedly while waiting in line at the grocery store checkout. As I was putting my groceries on the belt, tunnel vision came over me. I felt very lightheaded, dizzy, and nauseous, and my heart was racing. I had to steady myself with the cart, and the cashier called a clerk to bring me a glass of water, but I couldn't wait and rushed out of the store leaving everything on the belt. I was so embarrassed and scared! After that episode, I was so afraid it would happen again, and I started to do things that I thought would prevent it from happening again. It was a hot summer day, so I avoided heat. I was standing in line, so I avoided lines. I had eaten little that day, so I made sure I always had snacks with me. I felt nauseous, so I wouldn't leave home without Tums in my purse. I had an arsenal of safety and control measures, and it was awful to live that way."

Here are some common beliefs that go along with a panic attack: *I'm going to:*

- go crazy
- lose control
- have a heart attack
- die
- pass out
- choke or lose breath
- embarrass/humiliate myself

Common fears and triggers are:

- public speaking
- crowds
- flying
- open spaces
- medications
- illness
- heights
- driving/riding/traveling
- socializing
- working
- shopping, being in stores, waiting in lines
- not being able to leave

Common Behaviors

- avoiding situations
- leaving situations
- efforts to control situations

You might be wondering, *What if I don't have panic attacks?* Not everyone experiences the intensity of a panic reaction. In my opinion, this is because they are either not having the physiological sensations, or they are but they are not attributing danger to those sensations, such as the belief that they are losing control, going crazy, or dying. If you do not have panic attacks but rather consider yourself a "worrier," then you will probably relate to that feeling of constant unease rather than to a panic attack, that feeling of not being comfortable in your own skin. You likely feel that you are on hyper alert all the time.

The most important thing I want you to know is that although excessive anxiety is extremely distressing, it is not immediately dangerous. Long-term stress, however, has been shown to decrease our immune system and lead to stress-related illnesses, so I am so glad you are taking this step to alleviate it now. Remember:

It is very important that you consult with your doctor before assuming you are experiencing excessive anxiety. You always want to rule out medical conditions first. Many symptoms of anxiety can be mistaken for other medical conditions. Please see your doctor before beginning this program.

Convicted! How Did I Get Here?

Anxiety, the Condition

"First we make our habits; then our habits make us."

—Charles C. Noble

So how did we get here, locked up in our anxiety prison? Current research finds that anxiety "disorders" run in families and that they have a biological basis. They may develop from risk factors such as genetics, brain chemistry, hormones, personality, and life events. All are absolutely relevant. But, for the purpose of this book, we are going to focus on things we *can* control. Although your anxiety challenge feels like it's driving you, you will see that you are the one behind the wheel.

Be Aware: Anxiety is a "condition," but not in the way you might think. What if I suggest to you that anxiety isn't a disorder at all but rather a "condition." A conditioned response, that is. Earlier I explained that when we perceive danger, we respond naturally with fear. But if our fear response gets kicked off when there is no danger, we develop a "fear of the fear" and that creates much anxiety. Remember, anxiety is an emotion. Some emotions feel great and some not so much. Emotions supply us with important information. They are messages that we need to pay attention to. An emotion like anxiety, obviously, is one that does not feel good. But instead of heeding the important message of this emotion—which is to alert us to danger or to prepare ourselves—we choose to run from it instead. It is our natural survival instinct to avoid pain at all costs, and avoid we will! We will squash those "negative" emotions—distract, bury, stuff, avoid, and numb them. And we will do so in various ways, such as with drugs, alcohol, and food—anything to avoid feeling emotional pain.

Can we become emotionally exhausted? Yes. Can our emotions get the better of us? Absolutely! But a disorder? I say *no*! Anxiety is an *emotion*, and emotions are not disorders. Again, I am not saying there is no such thing as mental illness. But I do not think that experiencing excessive anxiety is a mental illness. What if emotions are in our control? What if you understood that emotions have a behavioral component? Now, I don't want to minimize emotions to make it sound like they are just mechanical; they are not. They are full and vibrant and a blessing that makes us know we are alive! But, if emotions are also behavioral, then that means a lot for the solution. And if they are behavioral, then what happens when we repeat behaviors again and again? They become habits. We all have good habits and bad habits. Habits can become strong; we get *conditioned* and really good at them. Think of going to the gym. At first it might be a difficult task, but the more you do it, the easier it becomes. In fact, if you go to the gym consistently and enough times, you will eventually do so with ease and actually miss it when you don't go! *That* is the power of habit.

So I describe anxiety as a "condition," because it is an emotion, and emotions are behavioral, and behaviors can become habits—a conditioned response. Let's look at the gym example again. What happens if you work only your upper body muscles? You will become *overdeveloped* in your upper body. We need *all* our muscles, yes? Wouldn't it make more sense to have a total body workout? Let's consider that our emotions are muscles too. When we overwork our anxiety muscle—although a very necessary muscle—it doesn't create the results we are looking for, and we risk becoming emotionally unfit. For optimal emotional fitness, as with optimal physical fitness, it's best to use and shape all of our muscles!

I use the physical fitness metaphor to describe emotions, but actually emotions are literally very physical. For example, slumping in your chair can make you feel tired, but if you sit up straight and take a big deep breath you can uplift your mood. The mind and body influence each other. You already know this, but you're probably not in the habit of thinking about it consciously. This is what awareness is all about—bringing things to your present conscious attention. When you do that, you will have a choice in what you do and therefore what you feel!

Try the simple exercise. Find some privacy and a comfortable place to be, and listen to or read the following. You will also want to get your journal for writing after the exercise.

#1 What emotion are you feeling right now? _____
#2 Rate how much you are feeling this emotion 0-10. Zero equals not at all to ten, the most you have ever felt it.
Proceed with the following: http://bit.ly/feartofreedomexercise (Use this link to hear the audio)

> Right now, I invite you to stand up or sit up as tall as you can. Physically hold yourself up, shoulders back. If you can, shake your body; go ahead and shake, dance, jump, bounce, toss your hair. Whatever you do, just move right now. And while you're doing this—this is really important here—I want you to smile. Smile big! Laugh! Even if you have nothing to laugh about right now—even if you don't have anything to smile about. Yes, you may feel a little silly. That's okay!
>
> What are you feeling now? Are you experiencing a different emotional state than before? Are you at least feeling more energy in your body?
>
> Okay, next, we are going to slow it down. So just breathe softly, a slow deep breath in and nice slow release out. If you are reading this and you are not driving, you can close your eyes, and if it feels good, hold your arms up like a big Y, reach for the sky, and smile. Hold your body tall, shoulders back, head slightly up. Smile! Smile as you lower your arms down to rest comfortably on your lap, or hands in prayer at your heart center, taking slow and deep calming breaths. Now, as you inhale, think the word *free*,

and as you exhale think or speak the word *release*. Releasing all that does not serve you. Releasing all the self-doubt, all of the stress. Nothing matters right now but this very moment. Try giving the words a color. Imagine that color breathing into your body, calming you as it hits every part of you. As you exhale, you are releasing all the tension. Imagine it leaving your body, releasing all that does not serve you. Give yourself a minute or two to feel what you are feeling. When you are ready, open your eyes; wiggle your toes and fingers.

How was that for you? What emotion are you feeling right now? My intention was that you lead yourself to a good-feeling emotion. If you were already in a good state, maybe it intensified. But maybe that didn't happen for you. Whatever emotions you experienced, identify them and write them in your journal. There is no right or wrong emotion.

The takeaway from this exercise is to demonstrate and become aware of how we create our emotional states behaviorally through our physical bodies. When you were jumping up and down and shaking it off, laughing and smiling, perhaps you felt silly, excited and energetic. Then when you slowed yourself down by sitting quietly, still smiling, perhaps you felt peaceful and calm. We *call* our emotions to us, simply by movements of our breath and bodies. Here is another example. Say we are in a room full of people, and I ask you to identify three people who are experiencing intense emotions and obviously not hiding their feelings. One person is feeling extremely angry, one is feeling extremely depressed, and another is feeling extremely anxious. After scanning the room, do you think you would be able to tell me whom I was talking about just by looking at them? They are not saying anything, but just by looking around the room could you point them out? My guess is you could. We naturally create our emotions with our facial expressions, body posturing, and breathing patterns. With this simple awareness, we can now choose to change our current state quickly and use it to build strong emotional muscle over time.

Put it to action: The next time anxiety spikes, slowly take a couple of deep breaths in, blow it out, smile, relax your muscles, and shake it off. *You might say to yourself, Thank you for showing up, anxiety, but I don't need you right now. I called you by mistake, but thank you for being a reliable friend!*

Breaking patterns of anxiety by inducing breathing, body movement, muscle tension, facial expressions, and posture is simple yet produces amazing results. You are sending messages to your brain and then triggering physiological responses. Choose your signals wisely! Smiling is actually sending powerful messages to the brain that everything is okay. Who knew a simple smile had so much power!

Next: Become aware of your power of thought.

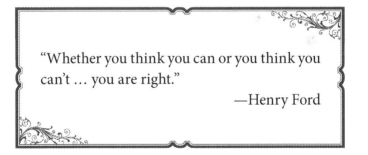

"Whether you think you can or you think you can't ... you are right."

—Henry Ford

The Thought/Mood Connection. Understanding that thoughts create how we feel literally stopped my panic attacks in their tracks!

In cognitive therapy we talk about three levels of thinking. At the surface, we have automatic thoughts (AT), thoughts that are in the forefront of our minds at any time. A deeper level of thought is our intermediate beliefs—our rules, attitudes, assumptions, and perceptions. And deeper yet are our core beliefs, global beliefs we have about ourselves, others, and the world; these thoughts tend to be more rigid and absolute. All levels of thinking create emotion. Let's dig into each level now.

Automatic Thoughts (AT): Some researchers suggest that the average person has seventy thousand thoughts a day. We are always thinking. Automatic thoughts or "self talk" consist of our choice of words, phrases, and questions. It is in our everyday thoughts that we can create our whole experience with just some choice words. What words, phrases, or questions make up your automatic thoughts? For example, how do you describe a plane flight? And isn't that just how you experience a plane flight? My guess is absolutely!

Our automatic thoughts are our mental self-talk. But it's not just the words, phrases, and questions we choose; it's also the *way* we say them, the tone, volume, inflection, and intensity. For example ask: "Why does this always happen to me?" Ask it first as if you were feeling sad and desperate: "*Why* does this *always* happen to *me*?" Now ask the same question, but this time ask it as a sincere, curious question: "Hey, why *does* this always happen to me?" Or, here is a common automatic thought: What if … Try going from *What if!!!* to *What if?* Or better yet, *So what if!* Feel the difference?

Our automatic thoughts also show up as images or pictures in our minds. Can you "see" yourself freaking out on the plane flight? The images we create in our minds are like movies we play out in our minds. These mind movies easily trigger our emotional state. Sometimes we play romantic or fun, easygoing movies that result in feeling good, and sometimes we conjure up stories and images resulting in unnecessary anxiety, panic, or worry. When it comes to anxiety, we are literally the creators of our own disaster films! We are acting as the screenwriter, the producer, and the lead actor! One of my favorite ways to explain this is: "We feel what we focus on all day long." But it's not *just* what we are focusing on; it's our beliefs and perceptions of what we are focusing on. Simply put, if you are *focused* on your future and you *believe* your future is promising, you will feel very differently than if you are *focused* on your future and you *believe* that your future is hopeless. Feel the difference? If you are feeling anxious, you are future-focused, picturing yourself in your mind's eye losing control in a certain situation that did not happen (imagined), or past-focused, remembering when you panicked and ran (real memory). These picture-thoughts trigger the emotion— in this case anxiety—and the physiological response in your body follows. It's worth mentioning here again: our bodies do not know the difference between what is real or what is imagined. Our thoughts determine the difference!

My Getaway CAR Worksheet will allow you to stop and call "Cut!" so you can rethink and change the scene of your movie.

You now see that our automatic thoughts are powerful! Since emotions come from our thoughts, we have to choose them wisely. Start to become aware of your automatic thought patterns and your power language. What are your trigger words, phrases, and questions? What are the words that you use that trigger anxiety for you? Typical AT patterns for me were: *OMG!* I still use it, but now I use it to enhance excitement, not enhance frustration! Other typical trigger questions were: *What if I pass out? What if I can't handle it? What if I make a mistake?*

Your turn: *Catch* and *shoot!* I thought of this exercise while exercising with Tony Horton's P90x program. He had a cardio move where you imagine catching a basketball then jumping and shooting the ball in the basket. I thought, *What a good idea for exercising your mind and catching those thought thieves!* Those anxiety-producing thoughts are robbing you of your right to freedom, your right for happiness! Don't let those little con artists get away with it! *Catch* those thoughts, write them on paper, and then *shoot* the paper in the wastepaper basket. Do it dramatically, like a basketball star! Rid yourself of any disempowering thoughts by putting them in the trash where they belong. Cap it off with a power word when you make the basket. *Hell yeah!* Or *Yes!* Or *Take that!* Or my personal favorite: *F that!* Here are some examples of thoughts you might want to slam-dunk. Later we will take the next step by challenging these imprisoning thoughts.

1. *I'll never have what it takes to get promoted at work.*
2. *I'm not smart enough to go back to school.*
3. *I can't feel good about myself until I lose weight.*

Intermediate Beliefs: Intermediate beliefs consist of our attitudes, rules, and assumptions, and they influence how we will react in any given situation. They are easily identified as *If … then …* statements and *meaning* statements. When it comes to anxiety challenges, these thoughts tend to be about perceived danger, vulnerability, and the belief in our ability to cope. Here were some of mine:

*If I show signs of nervousness, **then** people will think I am incompetent.*

*Not being able to control my anxiety **means** there is something wrong with me.*

*If my heart beats hard, **it means** I could be having a heart attack and I could die.*

Not one of mine, but a popular one I often hear:

*If I don't expect anything, **then** I won't be disappointed.*

Your turn: Identify your personal rules, attitudes, and assumptions, and connect the thought-mood connection even more!

1. _____

2. _____

3. _____

4. _____

5. _____

6. _____

Core Beliefs: Core beliefs are more rigid and absolute than intermediate beliefs, hence the name "core" beliefs. They are in our core, and we all have empowering and disempowering beliefs about ourselves, others, and the world. They are born in childhood and typically get induced by what we hear or infer from our elders. So if we were told as children that we were smart, lovable, and capable, then we probably will believe we are smart, lovable, and capable. If we were told otherwise, we might believe otherwise. These beliefs can come from our parents, teachers, or peers. They can be induced directly or indirectly. A child who was directly told he or she will never amount to anything might adopt the core belief: "I am not good enough." A teacher never directly saying a child is stupid—but displaying clear frustration with a child because he or she is not getting the lesson—might lead to that child adopting a core belief: "I am not smart enough." If a well-meaning parent tells people that her child is "just shy," that child may come to believe that is who she is. The bad news is that core beliefs are deeply rooted and the reason many of us stay stuck in our lives. We have core beliefs that hold us back. We can't move forward because of these beliefs. The good news is that a core belief is really just a thought, a thought that you have told yourself or heard so much that it turned into a belief. Haven't you ever believed something in the past that you no longer believe?

Of course you have! Just because you believe something doesn't mean it's true!

Your turn: Identify your core beliefs. Which ones are serving you? Which ones are not?

1. I am/I am not_____

2. _____

3. Others are/are not_____

4. _____

5. The world is/is not_____

6. _____

So let's break this down with a common fear-inducing event: speaking in public. I am using this particular event because I understand it is the most common fear humans have, *and* you know I have firsthand experience! I am going to make a guess that this is no stranger to you, either.

Automatic Thoughts (AT): *Oh no, I can't possibly do this. What if I fail? What if I stutter? What if I pass out? I'd rather die than give a speech! No way! Not doing it.*

Intermediate Beliefs: *If I show anxiety, people will think I am incompetent. If my heart beats fast, I am unsafe. If I can't do it, then I will be humiliated.*

Core Beliefs: *I am not capable. I am not smart enough. People will judge me. Others are judgmental.*

Doesn't it make sense that we might trigger a bit of anxiety with all these thoughts and beliefs? After all, our mind is just doing its job. This is our mind's way of protecting itself. It's the fight-flight-freeze response that we talked about earlier. By choosing these thoughts, we just pulled our internal fire alarm. However, like anything and everything, speaking in public is a "neutral event." It's life-changing to consider that *everything* is a neutral event. A roller coaster is a neutral event. Divorce is a neutral event. Even a natural disaster is a neutral event. In other words, it's just a meaningless thing by itself. But as soon as we attribute a meaning or a perception to something, it takes on that reality for us. A roller coaster can mean fun or it can mean danger. A divorce can mean failure or freedom. A natural disaster can mean all is lost or an opportunity for a new beginning. You get the idea of a neutral event. *So,* by giving public speaking the meaning of danger, we have just called upon our survival instinct— which naturally triggers a racing heart and shallow breathing. We now *focus* on the worst-case scenario, and we now *believe* we are not safe. We use intense, scary words, which in turn create greater intensity of our physiological responses, and we quickly find ourselves in panic mode. *Omg!* Now …

What do you do?

What are you most likely to do? What choice are you most likely to make regarding public speaking when you are feeling level-ten plus anxiety? Of course, if you are like me, you will *avoid giving a speech at all costs*! Yes, I was the queen of avoidance! I got quite good at it because I did it repeatedly. Remember, when you do anything over and over and over again, you master it. It becomes a habit. You are conditioning yourself to that behavior. I became very masterful and creative at avoiding. But what is the result of avoidant behavior?

An anxiety prison …

What initially happens when we avoid something that we fear? You know it: *relief!* Oh, that beautiful feeling of relief. And guess what? *You* called that emotion, too, just as you did the anxiety! How? Remember the previous exercise? In this case, too, the feeling of relief occurred because you took a big breath and instantly felt at ease. That's *you* changing your physiology by changing your breathing. Relief also occurred because you *told yourself* that you are now okay. Relief also occurred because you now *believe* that you are safe from a scary situation. In other words, *you* created the feeling of relief by changing your physiology, automatic thoughts, and beliefs. So, yes, what we do impacts our initial result—in this case, avoidance/relief. But what about the long-term? How does repeatedly avoiding situations impact our lives long-term? It creates a poor quality of life. It creates our tiny little cell. Repeating anything over and over conditions us. Avoidance becomes our safety net. But at what cost?

This is how I became incarcerated. How about you? We do this to ourselves over and over until it seems like it's just the way it is. That is one reason why it *appears* as though we don't have 100 percent control over our anxiety. We may have done anxiety for so long it is now on autopilot. It's becomes our "go to" emotion. It's similar to learning to drive a car. Eventually, we don't have to think about driving; our autopilot takes over.

The fear response may have started out of the blue with an unconscious thought, but the fear of the fear drove us to certain patterns of thoughts and beliefs that we keep repeating. And if someone also told us we have a disorder that we cannot control and will have to learn to cope with, now it sinks deeper and we begin to *identify* with the emotion. When we identify with something, it becomes us. It's no longer "I *feel* anxious"; it's "I *am* anxious." The result of that habitual pattern and self-identification is that we make our world smaller and smaller, until one day we are in that anxiety prison. How many opportunities have you missed because of avoiding? I have missed many opportunities for joy, growth, and connection. How do you think avoidance will affect your destiny, the result for your whole life?

So can you guess what the first part of the cure is going to be? You've got it: we have to *break* those thought and behavior patterns. We have to *break out* to *break through*!

Cognitive theory tells us that there is always a thought first. It may be a conscious thought or an unconscious thought that you are not readily aware of, but there is always a thought. So let's take the same neutral event, public speaking:

1. *The moment we give thought, we feel thought.* Have you ever known someone who loves speaking in public? There are people who seem to thrive on it and feel really excited about it. There are people who even do it for a living! What's the difference between someone who fears it and goes into a panic at the mere thought of it and someone who loves it? Are we born with a fear of public speaking or with a love of it? Of course not! *We* give it thought or a belief or a meaning! So remember, the person who fears it gave the meaning "worse than death!" But, what else could it mean? How about: "a great opportunity to help others!" So, with this meaning, what do you think one might feel? Excited to help others? Grateful for the opportunity? No wonder they love it! No wonder they now feel a different emotional state: excited! Interestingly, have you noticed that fear and excitement actually share many of the same physiological responses? Again, your body doesn't know the difference between the fear and excitement; only your mind does. The meaning you put to things, the perception you give it, is different. One of my favorite ways to change how I feel is to change my meaning: "I'm not nervous—I'm excited!" Your body knows not the difference!

2. *Emotional states affect what we do: our behaviors, choices, and decisions.* No wonder this person chose to accept the opportunity. It's exactly the opposite decision of avoidance, the previous behavior chosen when in a fear state. But a decision like this can be made *only* in an empowering state. Think about it. Can you remember a decision you made that you regret? What state were you in at the time? Now, we cannot guarantee that we will always make the "right" decision just because we were in an empowering state at the time, but you will definitely increase your chances of making the best one if you are. I always advise people— and I am advising you now—*never* make an important decision when you are feeling fearful, tired, angry, or any other disempowering emotion. I am not talking about real danger here, of course. When you are in *real* danger, that fear is needed, as our necessary survival alert. So, now that this person is accepting opportunity, remember …

3. *What we do impacts both our initial result and the quality of our whole life.* Initially, accepting opportunity may lead to feeling excited and hopeful. In the long-term it could mean opportunities for growth in all areas of life. But the ultimate long-term result is *freedom*, breaking out and breaking through to freedom from anxiety!

Neutral Event: Public Speaking

Meaning: Worse Than Death
Emotion: Anxiety
Action: Avoidance
Result: Initial relief short-term, tighter security prison long-term.

Meaning: Opportunity
Emotion: Excitement

Action: Think about what I want to say and how it will help others.
Result: Likely initial anxiety short-term, ultimate freedom long-term.

Because this book is about breaking through anxiety, we used anxiety for our sample emotion, and I encourage you to use this for any and all emotions. This is what you need to become emotionally fit! And here is the best news: are you starting to realize that *you already know this*? You do! It's just that it hasn't been in the forefront of your awareness. Once you are aware, you can make a conscious choice to create the change you want.

Awareness is the first key.

You already hold the keys to your anxiety prison. The problem has been that you have not been fully aware that you have them or been shown how to use them. *You* are the master set; *you alone* possess these keys. Once you own that, you can choose to unlock the gate and set yourself free.

Recap:
- ❖ Anxiety is a normal and necessary emotion. It helps us if there is real danger by triggering the fight/flight/freeze response, and it reminds us to prepare for something.
- ❖ Give thanks! Thank goodness for the gift of anxiety, as it keeps us safe and sound when necessary and pushes us to action when needed. You are not going crazy or going to die of some serious illness. That is your fire alarm going off when there is no fire.
- ❖ We have control of our breathing and posture, and the fire can be put out with changing our breath and physiology.
- ❖ Thoughts create how we feel, and emotions make it real. If you change your thoughts, you change the game.

This week you will play with the power of your thoughts. For this first key, Freedom for Your Mind, I have three tools that I initially used to break out of my anxiety prison all those years ago. Have fun, experiment, and gain awareness. Get to know yourself, and empower yourself not just by intellectualizing this but also by really experiencing it. Please remember, you can't just read this material. You have to *do* the material!

In the introductory homework, you clarified your Point A and Point B. You snapped your mug shot and knew exactly where you were on this journey—and you know what freedom would look like for you on the outside. Now it's time to get serious and …

Feel Your Freedom!

Affirmations On Fire! Cards

Affirmations are effective, but simple affirmations are not enough. I call mine *Affirmations on Fire!* because it's not enough to read them or even say them; you have to believe them, and you have to *feel* them! I have used them for years, and I continue to use them. When the statement becomes my reality, I make new ones! They definitely have worked for me in all areas of my life. Now it's your turn.

Use 4 x 6 index cards, so you can carry them with you. Here's how to make your own personalized cards:

A. On one side of the card, write what you want. Your Point B homework will give you great ideas.

"I want to feel confident."

B. On the other side of your card, write the statement in the present tense and in the first person, reflecting how you already have what you listed. For example, "I am approaching life with confidence!"

☀ Freedom Tip: "I am" statements such as the one above are the most powerful, but if stating "I am" is just too unbelievable for you right now, start with "I am becoming." Be sure to switch when ready. For example, "I am becoming confident in my life." "I am learning to face my fears with confidence." "I am becoming fearless!"

Keep the cards with you at all times. Use Post-it notes to post where you will see them, such as on your bathroom mirror. Say your Affirmations on Fire the first thing in the morning and many times during the day. *Essential*: Say it like you mean it! Say it as if you believe it *now*, even if you don't. Put emotion into it. Remember, they are called Affirmations *on Fire!* cards.

Focus on what you want and how your life would look, and allow yourself to *feel it right now*. This step is really important, because it takes more than motivation for lasting change. Motivation is about pushing yourself to do something, but remembering your *why*, and using your Affirmation On Fire cards to feel your best will pull you forward. Isn't it much easier to be pulled toward something than to have to push all the time? *Yes*! Next, it's time to ...

See Your Freedom!

Freedom Board

Your Freedom Board is a very powerful and fun tool used to turn your wants to reality. Think about this: everything that exists was first a thought! Thoughts become things! This comes from law of attraction philosophy. Like Affirmation On Fire Cards, I use Freedom Boards regularly in my life. Here is how:

Start collecting pictures, phrases, and words of things that you want to create in your life. Find pictures or words that represent that for you. It's also fun to use your own photos. Find mementos that mean something to you that represent your future life outside of anxiety. If you are fearful of public speaking, but you want to public speak, find a picture of a confident presenter and pin it. Whatever imprisons you, find a picture for what you want instead. Create your board and hang it where you will see it. You can use a corkboard or a video board. I actually use both and have specific boards for various goals.

Look at your board daily. This is a great exercise to do with your kids as well. Envision your future freedom! Now, is a good time to …

Fuel Your Freedom!

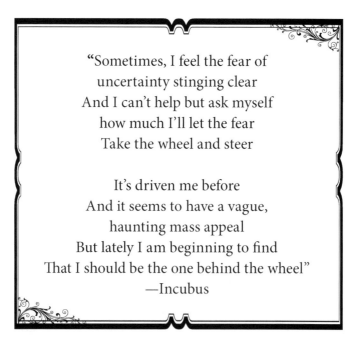

"Sometimes, I feel the fear of
uncertainty stinging clear
And I can't help but ask myself
how much I'll let the fear
Take the wheel and steer

It's driven me before
And it seems to have a vague,
haunting mass appeal
But lately I am beginning to find
That I should be the one behind the wheel"
—Incubus

Getaway C-A-R Worksheet

To escape anxiety state prison, you must have a fast, high performance getaway C-A-R!

You must learn to ...

C- atch the low octane thoughts that fuel low-quality emotional performance. Then,
A- nalyze Test the current quality of your choice of gasoline. And finally,
R- efuel by replacing any low octane gas with high octane for a well-fueled, high- performance emotional vehicle.

Remember, you may be a student driver, but with focus and persistence in no time you will be operating on auto-drive. Let's begin your driving lesson.

The C-A-R worksheet located in the back of this book will walk you through the thought/mood connection. This practice in cognitive awareness was what stopped my panic attacks in their tracks! I have included a blank worksheet and two samples to use as a guide. Before you begin using this tool, it's important to acknowledge that we have emotions for a reason. It's natural for us to want to avoid pain, so we will sometimes sweep painful emotions under the rug, numb them out, or deny them. Done safely, this is a necessary and helpful defense mechanism in the short-term. However, it is important to differentiate a defense mechanism that people often use in traumatic situations from what we are working on here. Here we are talking about when we misperceive events. It's not about *never* experiencing anxiety or any other emotion; it's about paying attention, heeding the message of anxiety, and the ability to know the difference between necessary and misfired anxiety.

So, when answering the question on the worksheet: "What else could this mean?" it's important to remember that. You will start to find that 99.9 percent of the time you are not seeing it right, misperceiving someone or something, letting your insecurities run the show. But it's also important to remember that there will be those times when you *are* right. Someone *was* being mean; they really *were* being a jerk, etc. This is not about putting a flower on a piece of dog poop! It's not about positive thinking. It's about checking your perceptions. This is why you will see two different outcomes on the CAR worksheet. Outcome #1 when you conclude you *are* misperceiving and creating unnecessary emotional responses or Outcome #2 for those times when the crap is undeniable. If you do find that your perceptions are actually spot-on, then it gives you pause to consider what to do about it rationally and reasonably. Remember, our emotions affect our actions. If we evaluate a situation and determine that we were right the first time, we now have time to consider what to do about it from a state of courage or peace or confidence or love and *then* determine what to do at that point. Thought records are a powerful cognitive tool and one that you will find useful for a lifetime. I don't need to use them regularly now, but I sure will whip out my CAR worksheet every now and again!

Important: Out of your head and onto the paper! Write it out! Don't do the CAR exercise only in your head! Eventually this skill will become second nature, but writing really conditions it creating the habit much faster than just trying to do it in your head. Eventually you will not need to write them out, because it will become your new automatic way of thinking. You will have this tool for a lifetime.

Key #1 Escape Plan:

Create your Affirmation on Fire! cards. Carry them in your purse, pocket and/or phone. Use sticky notes to post them and read them daily.

Create your Freedom Board.

Complete at least three CAR worksheets a week for at least sixty days.

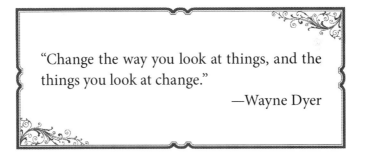

"Change the way you look at things, and the things you look at change."

—Wayne Dyer

After practicing for a week or two, write a paragraph about what this quote from Wayne Dyer means to you. How does it relate to what you just learned for Key #1? What has this meant in relation to your anxiety challenge? How can you use this in your life now?

Recommendation: I highly recommend that you do not continue on to Key #2 until you've had some success decreasing anxiety with Key #1. If necessary, please review the material and keep practicing. Remember, this may be completely new to you; be patient with yourself. You *will* get there!

Congratulations! You have just completed Key #1. If you continue to use and practice the tools and skills you just learned, they will serve you not only now but also for the rest of your life. These tools and skills are something you want to become second nature. Emotions that feel good will become your new "go to" emotions, because those are the emotional muscles you are now working! So continue working those muscles, and you will become more and more emotionally fit, experiencing more of the emotions you want to feel and less of the ones you don't. Remember, it's not about *never* experiencing anxiety or any other emotion; it's about paying attention, heeding the message, and understanding the difference between necessary and misfired anxiety.

Next, we will be addressing how food, toxins, and substances affect our moods and how we can nurture our bodies with the right foods, supplements, and physical activities to achieve optimal emotional health.

KEY #2 FREEDOM FOR YOUR BODY

From now on you will use the first key, because you understand that we literally *feel* what we *think,* that our mind-set is an essential factor for the challenge and for the cure. Now you will add the second key to experience that what and how we *eat* and how we care for our bodies is also monumental for feeling emotionally fit and healthy. Food, supplements, avoiding toxins, and exercise can be used not only to eliminate your symptoms but also to help you gain much-needed energy and vitality that may be blocking you from experiencing joy in your life.

The Food/Mood Connection

One panic attack I distinctly remember occurred during my hairstylist days while working on a client. Yes, as I mentioned in my story, I believe anxiety showed up unconsciously to let me know it was time to move on from my latest career choice, but I also think it had something to do with the whole pot of coffee I had just consumed, which was usual for me at the time (jeez, Peg, ya think?). That day I quit caffeine cold turkey. Fortunately, I never went through caffeine withdrawal like I know some people do. I just knew that coffee meant "that feeling," and I was *done*!

Another major attack occurred in a store while cashing out. While standing in line, I suddenly had tunnel vision. I felt dizzy and my initial automatic thought was: "People will see me lose control!" But what *triggered* the dizziness was the fact that I had been out in the sun drinking a glass of wine and not had much water to drink. I immediately quit drinking wine. I stayed out of the sun and drank more water.

This is why a holistic approach is important. It's not enough to recognize the thoughts. In both cases above food and/or environmental conditions brought on physiological symptoms that triggered fearful thoughts, *and that* led me to a full blown panic attack.

Today, I am able to again enjoy coffee and wine—just not a whole pot and just not out in the sun without water! Today, I am much more conscious about staying hydrated and monitoring my caffeine consumption. But those experiences showed me that what we ingest— and even what we *don't* ingest—can powerfully impact our moods and become triggers for panic and anxiety.

I am going to detail what foods are best to feel *your* best inside and out …

The Gut/Mood Connection

Your gut is in your head! The brain and the gut communicate in both directions and there is more and more research about our "second brain" and the digestive system's role in the production of serotonin, the body's natural feel-good hormone. Serotonin is an amazing hormone that regulates aggression, appetite, cognition, mood, sexual behavior, and sleep. Interestingly, 90 percent of serotonin receptors are found in your intestines, not your brain!

Serotonin, a neurotransmitter, is manufactured in our bodies from the amino acid tryptophan, which is derived from the food we eat. Diet, then, not only influences the state of our digestive system and overall physical health but also has a profound impact on memory, mental clarity, mood, and even the foods we crave; these functions are all regulated by serotonin.

Optimal nutrition and digestion, then, are crucial to the production and function of serotonin. Our bodies require serotonin as well as tryptophan, the amino acid from which it is manufactured.

Foods that may balance serotonin levels:[1]

- Foods rich in calcium, magnesium, and vitamin B to help with serotonin production.
- Fresh, organic fruits and vegetables.
- Black currant seed, borage, evening primrose, and hemp seed oils.
- Healthy complex carbohydrates and proteins.
- Bananas, kiwis, pineapples, plantains, plums, tomatoes, and walnuts are foods in which completely formed serotonin can be found.
- Foods rich in tryptophan include almonds, bananas, beans, peanuts, and soy foods.

Probiotics

---

1 "Healthy Digestion and the Secret Role of Serotonin." Last modified July 1, 2013. http://www.puristat.com/braingut/serotonin.aspx

Gut bacteria are affected in number and metabolic activity by stress—one more reason to keep stress levels down. A lack of critical gut bacteria leads to overproduction of stress hormones. Research by neurobiologists at Oxford University found preliminary evidence of a connection between gut bacteria and mental health in humans. The researchers report that supplements designed to boost healthy bacteria in the gastrointestinal tract (*prebiotics*) may have an anti-anxiety effect, as they alter the way people process emotional information. Probiotics consist of strains of good bacteria, while prebiotics are carbohydrates that act as nourishment for those bacteria.

Probiotic supplements, cultured vegetables such as sauerkraut, and coconut kefir all contain living probiotics (good bacteria) that will nourish your second brain and help clean out the toxins.

The Inflammation/Mood Connection

Because some of my clients take psychotropic medications, they might already understand some about how neurotransmitters like serotonin work to alleviate their symptoms. But almost none of them have heard how inflammation impacts emotional health. Traditionally, doctors are trained that inflammation is involved in autoimmune diseases like rheumatoid arthritis or Crohn's disease. Now science is revealing how important inflammation is in how it affects the brain, impacting us emotionally as well.

It's important to remember that—like stress and anxiety—inflammation isn't always a bad thing. Inflammation over a short period of time can be necessary for the body to break down damaged tissue to heal and regenerate. However, also just like stress, if it's long lasting it can spread and do damage to healthy cells and tissue.

Here are some of the most common inflammatory triggers:

- environmental pollutants
- chemicals in our water
- pesticides on our vegetables
- growth hormones and antibiotics in meat and dairy
- chemicals in our cosmetics
- preservatives in our food
- stress

Later in this chapter, I will share what I use to eliminate chemicals and minimize environmental pollutants.

The Supplement/Mood Connection

There is much debate over whether one should or should not take supplements. I used to think that supplements were absolutely necessary for good health. But since I have been eating more whole foods and live a plant-based lifestyle, I am confident that most of my nutritional needs are met through food. One caveat, however. I also know that it's not just what you eat; it's what you absorb. There are various reasons one may not be absorbing all the necessary nutrients from food. To be on the safe side, occasionally I still take a whole food based multivitamin, Vitamin D, and B12.

In this section we will look at vitamins and minerals that some experts believe may be effective for mood health. *Again, it is essential that you check with a health care professional before taking supplements.* Deficiency or overuse is nothing to ignore. When I work with clients, I always highly encourage them to discuss with their doctors the necessity of blood work to make sure their levels are optimal, especially for vitamins B and D, zinc, and iron. Deficiencies in these vitamins may cause one to feel anxious, depressed, or fatigued.

If you do decide to take a multivitamin or any other supplement, make sure it is free of fillers and artificial ingredients.

B vitamins: They don't call the B vitamins the stress vitamins for nothing! B1, B2, B6, and B12 are good-mood powerhouses. They have been known to boost energy levels, help control blood sugar, and ease fatigue, insomnia, irritability, and fight stress and PMS symptoms.

Vitamin B food sources: almonds, beans, bananas, legumes, whole grains, potatoes, dark leafy greens, and sea vegetables, such as seaweed, nutritional yeast, and kelp.

A special side note about B12: It is essential that we all get adequate vitamin B12, but contrary to popular belief you do not need to eat meat to get it. The truth is that no animal makes Vitamin B12. It's made by bacteria in soil and water, and the animals absorb bacterial B12 in their muscle. The cow didn't actually make it.

Magnesium and calcium: Both magnesium and calcium are known to have a calming effect on the body. They are often taken together, as they balance each other. Taken at bedtime, they can promote restful sleep.

Magnesium and Calcium food sources: spinach, turnip greens, sea vegetables, collard greens.

Magnesium food sources: oats, quinoa, legumes, nuts, and seeds. Herbs such as peppermint, cayenne, paprika, chamomile, and fennel.

Calcium food sources: broccoli, leafy greens, tahini, basil, thyme, and cinnamon.

Vitamin C: Protects against toxins, helps prevent damage of free radicals. That is why Vitamin C has been recommended if exposed to toxins produced by high stress, smoking, or alcoholism.

Vitamin C food sources: citrus fruits, guava, red and green peppers, grapefruit, kiwi.

Vitamin D: I was deficient in vitamin D. Vitamin D is naturally produced when we are in the sun, so it makes sense that people who live in winter regions may be more susceptible to deficiency. Make sure your Vitamin D level is optimal to sustain good energy, mood, and overall health.

Zinc: Zinc is important for nervous system function. Zinc is depleted by stress and excessive sugar consumption.

Zinc food sources: whole grains, beans, chickpeas, seeds, nuts, miso, cashews, almonds.

Iron: The most notable symptom of iron deficiency is fatigue. Iron is essential for the regulation of cell growth.

Iron food sources: spinach, raisins, nuts, beans, lentils.

When it comes to food and supplements and all the ways they can affect our mood and health, learning everything there is to know is confusing, time consuming, and overwhelming! But, *one* thing is for sure …

Prison Food is SAD!

I personally believe that the way we Americans typically eat, the SAD way, (Standard American Diet) contributes not only to mood challenges but also to our overall health. In fact, I truly believe we are slowly killing ourselves by the way the majority of us eat. I know that this may sound dramatic to some of you, but the evidence is stacking up. The good news is that I also believe we can begin to heal ourselves with food. I believe without a doubt that what we eat impacts our physical, emotional and even our spiritual state. My family and friends will often hear me say, "That's poison!" Or, "That's not food. That's a food-like substance." It's said with humor, but they know I mean it. Next, you will see an example of a typical anxiety inmate's diet that consists of food that could be contributing to keeping many of us feeling anxious, depressed, irritable, and physically sick—not to mention keeping us fat and tired! This chapter is intended to give you a basic idea of the food/mood connection. Let's start by looking at the biggest food offenders for anxiety:

Caffeine: I know, I know—not my *coffee*! There is so much confusing advice; some say coffee is good for you, and others say it is not. Regardless, one thing is for sure: it can definitely trigger anxiety! Too much can result in restlessness, insomnia, headaches, fatigue, and irritability. And it's addictive. Caffeine can be found in coffee (there's a small amount in decaffeinated as well), all teas except herbal teas, chocolate, some over-the-counter pain medications, soda, "energy drinks," and caffeine tablets.

Refined Carbs and Sugar: Refined carbohydrates such as white pasta and white rice spike our blood-sugar levels and deplete important B vitamins, which are essential for emotional health. Besides obviously being in doughnuts, cookies, cakes, soda, and candy, sugar is commonly added to ketchup, peanut butter, cereals, breads, soups, and hot dogs. The list goes on. Other big offenders are sport drinks and store-bought vitamin waters that claim to be healthy but have many grams of sugar.

Diet Soda: Research suggests that artificial sweeteners may prevent us from associating sweetness with caloric intake. As a result, we may crave more sweets, tend to choose sweet food over nutritious food, and gain weight. It's a lose-lose situation, and *not* for your waistline!

Processed/unnatural foods: Anything in a box or a can is usually highly-processed with sodium, chemical additives, and artificial flavors and preservatives. Too much can increase blood pressure and create a vicious cycle of addictive cravings. If you can't pronounce an ingredient, chances are it's not good for you.

Animals: It is important for the public to know the consequences of eating animals (and their milk). It's no longer a secret that the animals are injected with hormones and fed a diet that is unnatural for them and solely for mass production. The public also needs to be aware of the cruelty the animals endure in the process of becoming food. When we ingest animals and animal products, we too ingest what they eat *and* the negative energy of the torture they experience. Cage-free and free-range options are not better. We don't need to eat animals.

Alcohol: Anxiety sufferers will often take to alcohol to quell their symptoms. I know *I* did! I remember wanting to go to an arts festival, but the crowds were a big anxiety trigger. The first place I went was the wine and beer tent. One glass of wine did the trick. But that is a dangerous game. Besides the danger of possible addiction, alcohol dehydrates the body and affects brain cells. Studies show that, as with drinking coffee, drinking alcohol in moderation is okay and even good for you; it's often promoted as a health benefit of the Mediterranean diet. While going through this program, I suggest you cut out the drinking for now, but if you are going to drink, be smart about it. Limit consumption. Seek help if you or others around you worry about your drinking.

Tobacco: No one is going to argue that smoking is extremely bad and highly addictive. I used to think that having a cigarette alleviated my stress and anxiety, but the opposite is actually true. Smoking increases blood pressure, which can trigger other physiological symptoms that trigger the anxiety cycle. If you smoke, please consider quitting for you and your loved ones.

After reading all about the prison diet, what are you thinking right now? Remember, our thoughts determine how we feel. If you're thinking: *This is too much to give up!* then you are probably feeling unmotivated or overwhelmed. If you're thinking: *Wow, I can't wait! This is really going to make a difference for me!* then you are probably feeling curious or excited! Take a moment to jot down some of your thoughts in your journal or complete a CAR Worksheet. Then come back and we will talk about what a *freedom lifestyle* looks like!

Freedom Lifestyle!

No deprivation! There is no *diet* here, only a vibrant life!

What's important is what you *add* to your meals, not what you deny yourself. This is not and cannot be about deprivation. Start by *adding* a salad or veggies to any meal. Think of it as the opposite of a diet. This is not a diet at all. It is your *freedom:* a new high-quality way of living that fulfills all of your mental, emotional, physical, and even spiritual needs. It's about living more every day: with more vitality, more energy, and more stamina. Think of it as adding versus subtracting, fulfillment versus deprivation. Use the guide below to get started on how to eat for freedom; you're going to love how you feel!

"If you're trying to release excess weight, fat-free diets don't work. The only diet I recommend is the "Crap-Free Diet."

Freedom to Eat!

Fresh Vegetables and Fruit: It disturbs me that organic, pesticide-free, hormone-free, and preservative-free food (real food) is more expensive than the junk that is so easily available. If you are someone who never (or rarely) eats fruits and veggies and budget is a concern, by all means eat conventionally grown fruits and veggies. That is better than none, and you have to start somewhere! Try locally-grown and in-season fruits and veggies. I also keep a list of Environmental Working Group's (EWG's) "dirty dozen" in my coupon book and always buy those organic. They also give you a "clean list" of foods that are not as "dirty" as the dirty dozen. This is a great way to start. Remember, it's about *adding* in, not necessarily changing altogether. When shopping, look for colorful food. An easy way to determine the nutrient content of food is to look at the color. Foods with rich, deep colors (think: blueberries, spinach, sweet potatoes) are high in phytonutrients and pack a mean punch for fighting inflammation.

Fresh is best, then frozen, then canned. Have fun! Salads can become boring if you just have iceberg lettuce, a cuke, and a tomato. Look in your local grocery store and check out the prepared salads; buy the ingredients you like, and make your own salads to save money. Homemade salad dressing is healthier, cheaper, and so easy to make. Another way to eat well and save money is to buy your veggies a couple times a week to avoid having to throw away old food.

Fast Freedom Tip: Happy seven. A study conducted by Andrew Oswald, PhD, of Britain's University of Warwick, concluded: "Happiness and mental health appear to rise with the number of daily servings of fruits and vegetables a person eats, peaking at seven portions."

Grains/complex carbs: Carbs are not the enemy! *Refined* carbs and sugar are. Avoid simple carbohydrates like white flour products and sugar. The boost they provide in serotonin levels is temporary and quickly followed by a crash. Switch to brown rice and pasta instead of refined white grains. Look for the word *unrefined* when shopping and stay away from anything *refined*. Unrefined brown grains are not stripped of all their nutrients. Try some grains you never tried before. I love quinoa and use it for meals at any time of day. You can make a warm breakfast cereal, a light summer salad, or a hearty dinner dish, all with one grain.

Bonus Good News! Brown rice, buckwheat, wild rice, millet, amaranth, and quinoa all are gluten-free!

Start reading labels. Stay clear of added sugars and preservatives. Applesauce is sweet enough, so why ruin it with added sugars? If the label says "sugar free," it means it has a sugar substitute. Look for "no sugar added" instead. "Fat free" is another to stay clear of. It doesn't mean the food is naturally fat-free, but rather that there is a chemical substitute or added sugar or salt. Foods labeled "natural" could also have added sugars.

Listen, I know you're not going to die if you ingest one candy bar. But eating processed sugar regularly is a path of destruction as far as I'm concerned. So what do you do? Fruit is a winner! If you are going to have an occasional baked treat, make your own with a recipe that uses applesauce, dates, or other fruits for the sweetener. Stevia is also an option. Agave used to be considered an option for me, but because it's highly processed, I have eliminated it.

Protein: Beans, peas, and lentils are all legumes and are among the most versatile and nutritious foods available. Beans and legumes are a good source of protein and typically low in fat and high in fiber, folic acid, potassium, iron, and magnesium. You can buy them dried and soak your own, but if you are just starting out or are time-constrained, buy canned and experiment. Other great sources of protein include avocado, broccoli, spinach, nuts, and seeds.

Fast Freedom Tip: Spice up your life with turmeric! Touted for its natural anti-inflammatory benefits, use it to season savory dishes and even put a dash in your almond milk!

Choose Good Fat: We need essential fatty acids for brain health. Avocados, olives, nuts, and seeds contain essential fats. Omega 3 fats such as chia and flax seeds are great. Check the label, and stay away from hydrogenated or partially-hydrogenated fat. Coconuts and unrefined coconut oil are also good sources of fat.

Milk Does a Body Good: The nondairy kind, that is! There are so many options to non-dairy milk out there: almond, hemp, coconut, flax, hazelnut and cashew. Try them, and see what you like! As you learn and grow, you will want to make your own nut milks. It is super easy and avoids the additives typically found in store-bought brands. Check out my video where I show you how to easily make homemade almond milk: https://youtu.be/hTWageBTanY

Reduce inflammation with high-alkaline foods: We talked about the effects of inflammation on the body and ultimately your emotions. Highly acidic foods like dairy and meat can steal vital nutrients from your diet and push the body into a state of inflammation. Add in high-alkaline foods such as spinach, broccoli, cucumbers, celery, bell peppers, avocados, and lemons, and enjoy natural inflammation reducers such as exercise and weight loss.

A Smoothie a Day! I start my day with a green smoothie. This is a fast and fun way to get the much-needed energy and nutrients first thing in the morning. Check out my website for my 7-Day Smoothie Party to get you started!

Remember Variety: Change it up often. This ensures you won't get bored and that you get proper nutrients. Experiment and try different recipes using a variety of greens, veggies, fruits, grains, and legumes. Add color to your diet by mixing red, green, yellow, orange, and purple to your meals. Have fun with it!

Water, Water, Water! Get in the habit of carrying a non-plastic bottle of water with you at all times. Water doesn't have to be boring! Add yummies to the water (but don't add sugar). You can add anything you like: lemons, limes, and other fruits. I love using frozen berries. I also love cucumber water. Dehydration can cause fatigue and impaired coordination and judgment, and it can trigger stress headaches and even high blood pressure. As a good guide, drink half your body weight in water daily. Looking back, I'd bet many of my panic triggers were due to dehydration. How about you?

Fast Freedom Tip: remember to eat s-l-o-w l-y. Put all your focus on the smell, taste, texture, and sound of the food. Savor every bite. Eat mindfully. Savor your food and you may be amazed at how well you can emotionally ground yourself and improve your digestion just by this one habit!

Shop Outside: Consider shopping more in the outside aisles, where you will find produce (real food), and less in the middle aisles, where you will find boxed and prepared food. If something has an expiration date of 2099, it's a safe bet that it's full of stuff you don't want to ingest!

Adopt a Kind Lifestyle: Educate yourself about eating animals. If you are in New York or California, visit Farm Sanctuary. Have an open mind and an open heart. *If* you do choose not to eat animals, make sure you learn how to be a healthy vegan, not a junk-food vegetarian, as I unknowingly was for years. That is just as unhealthy!

Quit Smoking! If you smoke, I highly encourage you to take that step to quit. You owe it to yourself and your loved ones. Hey, you have come this far for freedom; if you can quit anxiety, you can quit smoking too!

Many of us take the power of food for granted. I believe the body has the power to heal itself much more than we give it a chance to. I became a certified health coach to learn more about this important information and to have the ability to help my clients in a greater and more holistic capacity. I am encouraged to see that today there is much more attention to the food/mood connection. Eastern medicine has always been on board, but finally western medicine is catching up. Movies and documentaries are spreading the news to educate people on this important information; *Forks over Knives*, *Food Matters*, *The China Study*, and *PlantPure Nation* are some to check out!

Freedom to Move!

Exercise is a must for anxiety relief. But I don't like using the word exercise, I prefer to use *energize*! I don't necessarily mean tough, hour-long sessions, but certainly go for it if that is what you enjoy. Moving is essential for emotional and mental health, because it releases endorphins, which can act as a natural stress reliever and antidepressant. It is known to increase serotonin levels naturally. A ninety-minute walk can increase levels by 100 percent. It's good for your body, because it will make your immune system strong and your body durable. It wakes up your spirit. In fact, I debated whether to place this section here or under the next section on unlocking freedom with your spirit! It can truly give you the energy to live life fully. I definitely know it if I miss too many days of physical fitness. I notice my energy and mood drops, my confidence wanes, and sleep is disrupted. That is a recipe for stress and anxiety!

Fast Freedom Tip: Remember the power of language? The words *exercise* or *workout* can have negative connotations and as a result consciously and unconsciously dampen our desire to move. Change your words—change your experience! Instead of: "I have to exercise (or work out)," try: "It's time to energize!" "Moving my body creates a well oiled machine!"

Below I cover my favorite ways to energize. I encourage you to find your way and, as always, *please consult with your health provider before beginning a new energizing regimen.*

Yoga: According to the *Harvard Mental Health Letter*: "Available reviews of a wide range of yoga practices suggest they can reduce the impact of exaggerated stress responses and may be helpful for both anxiety and depression. Indeed, the scientific study of yoga demonstrates that mental and physical health are not just closely allied, but are essentially equivalent. The evidence is growing that yoga practice is a relatively low-risk, high-yield approach to improving overall health."[2] Yoga is an integral part of my health regimen. It is good practice for "staying in the present," which is key to anxiety relief. I am reminded of one of my favorite quotes:

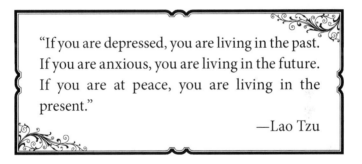

"If you are depressed, you are living in the past. If you are anxious, you are living in the future. If you are at peace, you are living in the present."

—Lao Tzu

Focusing on your breath, moving with your breath, and practicing meditation and deep relaxation all help to calm the mind and body. If I miss my practice for a few weeks, even while energizing in other ways, I can feel the difference emotionally. If you are interested in experiencing yoga, chances are there are classes where you live. If not, try a DVD or even a Youtube video.

---

2 "Yoga for Anxiety and Depression." Harvard Mental Health Letter, April 2009, http://www.health.harvard.edu/newsletters/Harvard_Mental_Health_Letter/2009/April/Yoga-for-anxiety-and-depression.

Aerobic and strength training: You can swim, bike, run, jog, ski, play sports, walk the dogs, play with your kids, and walk in sand, up mountains, or up the stairs! It doesn't matter what you do— just move! You can join a gym or use your own backyard. You can use high-tech machines, weights, and gadgets, or you can use the ultimate machine, your body! The possibilities are endless. There are videos with every form imaginable. I prefer to use DVDs, and in good weather I take it outside with the fur kids! No question, though—my ultimate favorite is dancing!

Dancing: I think dancing deserves its own category. It covers everything, unleashing freedom for mind, body, and spirit. You cannot be anxious in mind, neglectful of your body, or unhappy in spirit when you're dancing! Sadly, people get too concerned with how they look. Isn't it interesting, though, that as soon as a few drinks go down some people suddenly find the courage. To me that is proof that we are born to dance but are afraid and locking up our natural instincts. Don't rely on "liquid courage." Be free and dance like no one is watching!

One thing worth noting: When it comes to physical fitness, there is a lot of talk about what type is best, the most effective length of session, how many times a week is necessary, and what and when to eat. It can all be so confusing. I believe the body intuitively knows what it wants and needs. Experiment, have fun, test, and measure. Your escape plan this week will help you hone *your* best regimen.

Freedom to Sleep!

A sleep-deficient lifestyle counters your freedom lifestyle. When you don't get enough sleep your body goes into a state of "high alert" resulting in increased production of stress hormones and inflammation in the body. If you don't have trouble sleeping but choose to only get a few hours, I encourage you to reconsider. If you have trouble sleeping, you may have noticed sleep has automatically improved as your thoughts, food choices, and physical energizing have improved. This will be interesting to note in your journal.

What Else?

In addition to the basics: food, supplements, physical fitness, and sleep, there are drug-free treatment options available. I listed a few below, and I encourage you to learn more about your options and decide if any might be a fit for you.

Acupuncture: Acupuncture is an ancient Chinese treatment method. Traditional Chinese medicine believes that health is dependent on *qi*, which, in a person in good health, moves in a smooth and balanced way through a chain of fourteen main channels (meridians). By inserting needles into the points that belong to different meridians, we stimulate the body's energy (qi) to start the healing process and assist it to restore its natural balance.

Acupressure: Like acupuncture, acupressure is also an ancient Chinese healing method. But instead of applying needles to meridian points on the body, you apply pressure with your fingers and hands.

EFT (Emotional Freedom Technique or Tapping) I have been practicing EFT techniques myself and introducing it to my clients with great results. I particularly enjoy EFT because it combines the physical benefits of acupressure with the cognitive benefits of conventional psychotherapy. Instead of inserting needles or pressure to meridian points, light tapping on certain meridian points with your fingers is used along with self- talk to first release emotional and physical stress and then replace it with affirming and healing statements as you continue to work the meridians with the tapping process. It is easy to learn, and you can do it on your own or with a practitioner.

Chiropractic Care: *How does chiropractic relate to anxiety?* you might be asking. Well, thinking holistically, we learned that inflammation can affect mood, and NSAIDS are often taken to decrease inflammation. I was taking so much Advil when my back went out many years ago. I went to a wonderful chiropractor and was able to completely cut out the Advil. With chiropractic care I was able to eliminate the pain and damaging inflammation naturally. I believe chiropractic care is important not only for spinal health but also for proper alignment of our knees, feet, shoulders, and hands and can be extremely beneficial in stopping the degenerative process.

Serotonin Enhancers: Instead of pharmaceutical drugs, amino acids and other serotonin enhancers have been used to alleviate anxiety and depression.

- 5-HTP (5-hydroxytryptophan): According to studies published in *Eating and Weight Disorders* and other journals, this amino acid calms anxiety and lifts mood. It has also been known to reduce cravings and curb appetite.
- tryptophan
- St. John's Wort
- SAM-e (S-adenosyl-methionine)
- melatonin (to aid sleep)
- holy basil

Essential Oils: I also have been integrating aromatherapy with essential oils into my holistic psychotherapy practice. Aromatherapy also promotes the health of body, mind, and spirit. As noted by the National Association for Holistic Aromatherapy (NAHA):[1]

"It [Aromatherapy] seeks to unify physiological, psychological and spiritual processes to enhance an individual's innate healing process."

Very exciting indeed.

According to the *Reference Guide For Essential Oils*, by Connie and Alan Higley (2014 edition), oils that ease anxiety include: lavender, orange, lemon, Roman chamomile, valerian, melissa, copaiba, ylang, ylang, Bergamot, and Frankincense, just to name a few. Oils can be diffused into the air, simply inhaled directly, or applied to hands or a tissue. I personally have adopted an "oils lifestyle" for me and my family—including my fur kids. They are a great natural resource to incorporate toxin-free living from your body to your home. To learn more about my oils lifestyle and how you can have one too, feel free to visit my Young Living website at https://www.youngliving.org/peg11

Key #2 Escape Plan:

1. Daily Journal Recording

You will be able to track progress, but more importantly, you will begin to become aware of how food, supplements, and movement (or lack of these) are affecting your emotional and general health. What I have found most helpful is to journal every day during this program, starting first thing in the morning, and jot down anything that you notice throughout the day. What is your mood upon waking? Rate 0-10. What did you eat and what time? Did you exercise? What did you feel just after eating that donut? If you continue to journal for a couple of weeks, you will be able to notice certain patterns and connections between what you do and how you feel. You will also be able to look back and see your amazing progress, which will help keep you motivated, for sure!

Use the Institute of Nutrition's food plate along with your food journal to help you discover and create your best health regimen.

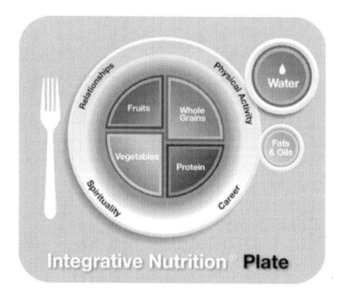

2. *And/or* go deeper and discover your food sensitivity blueprint:

Most of us have foods that our body does not process well. For me, that food is dairy. Growing up I remember always having to clear my throat. It wasn't until I became a vegan that I unexpectedly noticed that phlegm and congestion had disappeared. Most of us are unaware of these foods, because, like with me, they do not cause a full-blown anaphylactic allergic reaction like hives or our throat closing. However, eating them contributes to that low level of inflammation within our bodies. Some signs that you might have a food sensitivity are: fatigue, headaches, skin issues, chronic yeast, feelings of depression, achy joints, brain fog, bloating ... and much more. I offer my clients a whole food clean-eating cleanse based on an elimination diet and also provide a full 28- Day Plant-Based Transformation Program. In the cleanse, we take out the most common allergy-triggering foods for two weeks and then reintroduce it. You then have your own personal blueprint, and you know what works for you and what doesn't. You can request my DIY version of the cleanse at 50% off the regular price by providing proof of purchase of this book.

3. Commit to move! Choose some form of energizing that is fun and motivating for you and do it at least five to six times a week. Fun is required!

4. Research the alternative options mentioned in this chapter, and see if any might be a fit for you.

Congratulations! You have just completed Key # 2 of this program! You are creating a *new freedom lifestyle* by getting emotionally, nutritionally, and physically fit! Remember that mind and body work *together*. Emotions trigger hormones. Stress releases adrenaline. Prolonged adrenaline sets our cells up for inflammation, causing the potential for disease. Prison food promotes inflammation in our bodies. On the other hand, a freedom lifestyle promotes positive emotions and decreased inflammation—all resulting in the opposite effect, setting us up for outstanding health and happiness naturally.

Up next you will find how to insure you don't go back to that tiny cell any time soon!

KEY # 3 ☀ FREEDOM FOR YOU!

So now you know the how and why of panic and anxiety. You also know the mechanics: how your specific thought processes, physiological patterns, and health and wellness patterns contribute to or eliminate panic and anxiety symptoms. You now know how to escape Anxiety State Prison. But what about *staying* out? While writing my story it became crystal clear to me. *Yes*, understanding exactly what was happening to me and finding out I wasn't crazy was a relief in and of itself! *Yes,* practicing and challenging my thoughts and perceptions and creating a new health and wellness regimen was paramount to symptom reduction! *But* what I never was consciously aware of until years later was that the symptoms would always find their way back if I denied my *spirit.* Only when I allowed others to dim my light—only when my spirit was caged up, only when I was not allowing my light to shine to just *be* myself, my true self—did anxiety show up and keep showing up at key times in my life.

My intention for this book has always been to help people break through fears and break through to freedom. Freedom to live the life we *all* deserve. Freedom to be uniquely and authentically ourselves, with no apologies. But it wasn't until *after* I wrote my story that I could see that truth so clearly. Marianne Williamson said it best in her poem *from A Return to Love: Reflections on the Principles of a Course in Miracles:*

"Our deepest fear is not that we are inadequate. Our deepest fear is that we are powerful beyond measure. It is our light, not our darkness that most frightens us."

Give yourself permission to shine your light! It's the only way to really live with forever freedom! Next, you will learn what that means in every area of *your* life.

Primary Food: The Key To Lasting Change.

Again, you could escape your anxiety prison using only Keys #1 and #2. Remember, I obtained only Key #1 initially and was able to kick panic attacks completely. But if you want to greatly reduce your chances of getting yourself reincarcerated, you will absolutely need the last key. Key #3 is *primary food,* what it is, and why you must start growing this precious crop. Focus on this, and you will ignite your spirit, leaving excessive, life-sucking anxiety behind for good!

With Key #2, we talked about food, but the food we put into our bodies is really just one source of nourishment. What do you think of when I say primary food? You might think about the four food groups we were taught in health class. During my studies at Integrative Nutrition I learned that the food we eat is *not* primary food at all; it's actually secondary food. This is an empowering distinction and will make so much difference in your life. Secondary food is the literal food that provides the nutrients our physical bodies need, while *primary* food is the good stuff our spirit will thrive on. It's why we are here on this earth. These nutrients provide us with joy, meaning, and fulfillment. It is play, fun, romance, intimacy, love, achievement, success, art, music, self-expression, leadership, excitement, and adventure—these are the "foods" we need to *ignite our spirits*. We need to grow this food and tend to our garden with care and love.

The truth is that what doesn't grow *dies*. If you were working with me and you told me that you didn't feel fulfilled or that you didn't know what or how to fulfill your purpose in this life, I would know that you were not growing in some area of your life the way you wanted to be. This is exactly what was happening to me years ago by not pursuing my dreams. My anxiety challenges were their strongest when I was not pursuing my purpose. I didn't look at it that way back then as a spiritual purpose, but I now understand this to be true.

So what about you? It's not just about big dreams. It's about the whole circle of life.

What area in your life do you feel something lacking? Maybe you are growing well in your career but feel disconnected from friends and family and are feeling lonely. Maybe you are not where you want to be financially, and you know you have some spending habits you want to change. Maybe you feel your intimate relationship isn't where you want it to be because deep down you know you need to end it, or you haven't been nurturing your relationship the way you know you could be.

Any of these areas of our lives can become unbalanced, and let's be real—that is normal and sometimes unavoidable. In fact, I think we get ourselves into more trouble by trying to keep balance when balance can't really exist. Kind of like trying to control all things that can't be controlled! What we *can* do is tend to our lives. Our lives cannot be left unattended without repercussions. Just as a plant left unattended for too long—well, you know what happens! It's up to us to not just plant the seeds but also cultivate the soil.

Joy, relationships, health, spirituality, home environment, and more. This is what life is all about, my friends. This is your primary food. And if you put your energy and focus on these areas, you will automatically be crowding out the anxiety. It will become unnecessary. If you are choosing to nurture and grow in all these areas *and* choosing to give to something beyond yourself, imagine how you will feel. Just imagine the excitement and adventures awaiting you! You will finally see how important, needed, wanted, and special you always have been, and you will feel the love that may have eluded you, because you will be *giving it freely, and what you give always comes back to you.*

So now we have come full circle. Remember the beginning of your journey here with me when you identified your Point B? Recall that your Point B is not only *what* you want but also *why* you want an anxiety-free life. It's what that Point B will mean not only for you but also for others. With the circle of life exercise coming up, you will clearly identify what is off balance and then take action steps to get on course. But always remember that it's about the bigger picture, the bigger why.

I can't say this enough, because if you continue to focus only on *what* you want, you will continue to struggle with anxiety, because let's face it—anxiety is a selfish emotion! Anxiety is all about "what's wrong with *me?*": *What will others think about me? Do I look okay? Do I sound okay? Will they like me? What if they don't like me?* Blah, blah, blah. When I shifted my focus from inside to out—inner fears to the infinite outer possibilities of helping others—I experienced a whole new way of being. When I adopted what I like to call a pay-it-forward mind-set, I experienced life differently. It is so easy to do, and you are probably already doing it, but when you bring awareness and intention to it, it's that much more powerful. You will literally crowd out your anxiety and replace it with pure fulfillment. Train your brain to have a pay-it-forward mind-set, to have an "other outer focus." When you do, *you* will be the one who notices the elderly person who needs help getting something off the high shelf at the grocery store. *You* will be the one who notices the cashier having a bad day and make her laugh. You do this anyway at times, but without training your brain toward this "other outer focus" you have probably missed many opportunities because you had been inside your head—worrying and doing the negative mind chatter that was unknowingly creating all that anxiety to begin with! Having a pay-it-forward mind-set can also mean donating money to a cause, but it certainly doesn't need to. Speaking of causes, if you don't have one, I highly recommend you get one! My personal belief is that everyone is passionate about *something*. One of my passions is for non-human animals and educating us human animals about their peril and offering ways to create a kinder world for us all who live here on planet earth. What are you passionate about? What is important to you? *You* do matter, and your efforts are needed and important.

Now I must also mention the other end of the spectrum: giving of yourself *too much*. Many people can get wrapped up in giving so much that they neglect themselves. They are giving to their families, children, partner, friends, and church—just trying to do too much and giving no time to themselves. If this is you, stop it! Part of the reason you struggle with anxiety is that you are burning yourself out, and although it's beautiful that you are a loving and giving person, it is also costing you and actually the very people you are trying to support, because they are not getting the best of you. You owe it to yourself and your loved ones to stop overextending yourself.

Key # 3 Escape Plan:

Complete the Circle of Life exercise. In this exercise, you will identify imbalances in your "primary foods." In the beginning of this journey you wrote your Point B, what you wanted and what it would mean to you and the people in your life to actually be how you want to be. You planted your seeds. Now it's time to *create* the life you deserve by tending the soil! As you learned with Key #1, thoughts become things; this is true, but not without action. There are many areas to grow, so to make it as easy as possible:

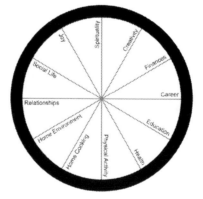

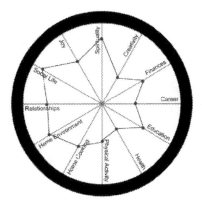

What does *your* life look like?

1. For each primary food category, identify what your 10 is. 10 is the outside of the circle and exactly where you want to be, your ultimate goal.
2. In each individual pie, identify where you are now from 0-10. 0=no achievement at it to 10=achieved. Place a dot in the piece of pie that signifies your number, and then connect the dots to see the shape of your wheel.
3. Identify just one action needed that will get you closer to your 10 for each category. You will have twelve actions total.
4. Write these actions and the benefit of them on your commitment statement below.
5. Prioritize these actions by scheduling them into your daily routine.
6. Practice the routine until it becomes your lifestyle. That will probably only take about sixty days of consistent action. That's good news compared to how long you have been living with anxiety habits!

Example:

1. Physical Activity: My 10 = Daily physical activity for at least thirty minutes.
2. Where am I now: Locate the dot using the 0-10 scale. My now # = 5.

3 +4. See commitment statement below.

5. Alarm is set a half hour early to walk dogs first thing in the morning.
6. Consistently remembering my *big why* has the power to keep me going and growing!

Commitment Statement

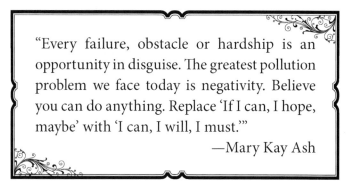

"Every failure, obstacle or hardship is an opportunity in disguise. The greatest pollution problem we face today is negativity. Believe you can do anything. Replace 'If I can, I hope, maybe' with 'I can, I will, I must.'"

—Mary Kay Ash

I, _____, commit to the following:

1. Walking the dogs for thirty minutes. This will lessen my anxiety, create health in my body and mind, and contribute to my dog's health and happiness too!

2.

3.

4.

5.

6.

7.

8.

9.

10.

11.

12.

Signed_____Date_____

⇨ Daily journal: every day list five things you are grateful for that day.

⇨ Daily journal: every day list five ways you gave to others today.

⇨ Next, write about how you would like to give. Do you have a cause? If so, how can you become more involved? Remember, it doesn't have to be grand scale. Maybe you have items that the Red Cross is looking for that are just collecting dust. If you do not have a cause, think about what you feel passionate about, and explore what's out there. If nothing exists in your area, who knows? Maybe you could start something yourself!

⇨ Here are some links to help you explore:

Find volunteer opportunities in your area: http://www.volunteermatch.org/

Adopt a pay-it-forward mind-set: http://.www.pifexperience.org/

You did it! You now own the three keys necessary to unlock your prison gate and break through to your personal freedom. Like Glenda the Good witch said: "The power was within you all along." True story! The power of awareness, the power of intention, the power of knowledge, and the powerful tools. You now know that *you* are the key to overcoming debilitating anxiety. You owned the keys all along. I just helped you to see them and use them!

Give yourself *huge* congrats, because I know this wasn't easy. It took courage, honesty, vulnerability, and commitment. You might have struggled with family members and friends trying to keep you in your old patterns. That can happen sometimes when people worry they will lose you because you are growing without them or beyond them. They might not be comfortable with this new side of you, but with love, understanding, and time, this can be overcome. On the other hand, sometimes relationships do change or even end. Through this process you have been up and down and all around; you have been testing yourself and stretching yourself. You may have been taking one step forward and two steps back. That, my friend, is just the true nature of progress. Just remember they are growing pains, and growing pains may hurt. But again, *what doesn't grow* …

Don't forget to complete your symptom assessment again to see how far you have come and determine where you still need to practice.

Oh, and don't be surprised if your anxiety returns every now and again when you are having one of those growth spurts. Remember that's just your old friend trying to keep you safe and sound in your comfort zone. Now you can gently tell your old friend: "Thank you, but I've got this one."

A Client's Breakthrough

The names have been changed to protect privacy.

I met with Marge for twelve sessions. Marge reported having trouble with anxiety periodically throughout her life. Lately, for the past three months, she reports daily panic attacks, a constant feeling of unease, trouble sleeping, and an overall feeling of discontentment. She could not identify any precipitating factors. Even though her chief complaint was anxiety, oftentimes her focus during our sessions was on her relationship with her husband. She had been married for a number of years, and her biggest complaint was that she felt bored, questioning if she had made the right choices in her life. She made progress in symptom reduction quickly in just the first few sessions with psychoeducation and effective breathing and mindfulness tools.

But it was during one session in particular, while discussing personal rules and beliefs, that she made a major breakthrough.

She realized that she had rigid rules for herself, which made it easy to conjure up anxiety, and also rules for her relationship, creating tension and chronic feelings of disappointment in her husband.

One rule Marge identified: "In order for me to feel happy and calm, I need to know my plan for the day and keep my routine."

I helped her understand that having a routine and a plan for the day is great—and I need that too—but when it becomes a rigid rule, something that has to happen to feel happy and calm, that's where we can get into trouble, because we don't have 100 percent control over the day's events.

She identified a second unspoken rule. With a little laugh, she admitted, "My husband also has to agree to follow my routine."

Of course, she was quickly able to see how these rules caused her own anxiety to increase not only in this situation but also generalizing and manifesting to other areas of her life. She also could see how it set her husband up for feeling pressured and unable to fully please her much of the time.

This created a pattern of anxiety for her *and* frustration and unhappiness in her marriage.

The next step was to see and understand the core *fears* underneath her rules. We did this by asking questions like: "What does it mean to you if you do not keep a routine? What does it mean if your husband doesn't follow your routine?" With these questions— and with follow-up questions such as "What is bad about that?"—ultimately, she was able to identify her core beliefs or core fears. "It means I am not perfect. It means I am not capable. It means I am not enough. If I'm not perfect, my husband won't love me."

It was powerful for her to realize her underlying fear, the core fear of not being enough and the fear of not being loved. It started to make complete sense to her. I also helped her understand how her fears actually have good intentions to keep her safe and sound but how they are not conducive to a fulfilling life or relationship.

Once she clearly connected her rules with trying to keep control (control that doesn't exist)—and understood that her efforts to keep that control not only did not protect her from her from her worst fears but actually perpetuated them—she was on her way to freedom!

I guided her through an exercise of listing simple and specific things that *were* in her control at any time—things she could do when feeling afraid she was not enough or not loved. When we take control of those things we can control and let go of the things we cannot, life suddenly becomes so much easier!

She listed many simple yet powerful self-loving behaviors from eating well and exercising to affirmations she created and carried with her, to simply giving herself a break to have a cup of tea. She also listed things she could do to experience love with others, such as contacting friends by phone or text and taking her kids outside to play. We also did another list specific to her husband. She listed ways to give love simply and meaningfully to him. This made her feel loving, playful, and flirtatious, feelings she had not felt for him in a very long time.

She prioritized reconnection with her husband and together they planned rituals similar to ones they had shared early on in their relationship. For them this included weekly date nights, a monthly local weekend overnight, and a plan to look forward to a bigger yearly romantic getaway together.

Marge's initial problem of anxiety alleviated itself to being almost non-existent. She went from daily panic attacks to zero. She also reports feeling happier with improved sleep and energy.

We all have rules and beliefs that limit our joy, happiness, and fulfillment in life. It's not until we can bring these rules to conscious awareness that we can see that they are really just fears. Fears that we can choose to annihilate, and when we do, we can make the breakthroughs that have been waiting behind walls of self-doubt, unhappy relationships, and dreams unfulfilled. It *is* possible to get on the other side of that wall. Your amazing life exists there. It *is* possible to break out of fear and break through to freedom.

What's Next:

You are on your way, *and* this is just the beginning. It's all about lifestyle changes to your whole self: your mental, emotional, physical, and spiritual health.

Through telling my story and sharing my personal escape route, I wanted to give you the first tools, the same ones I initially used to kick my anxiety to the curb. I wanted to deliver it with a personable feel, as if you're getting one-on-one, individualized help from me. But I know I can create that only so far in a book. With that in mind, I have created different levels of engagement. This book can be used alone, and you will be able to complete it at your own pace. But if you want more, below you will see that I have created fantastic options that will support you to take your growth to the next level.

Please remember just as we grow and change, so may my services! Please visit my website for my most current offerings.

1. Anxiety Breakthrough! A Holistic Emotional Mastery System: Dig deeper into the tools and strategies with online

individual home study programs and live group programs based on Peg's book *Anxiety Breakthrough! Break Out of Fear, Break Through to Freedom.*

2. VIP Day Retreat!
   Experience a *private*, custom-tailored one-day intensive of 1:1 coaching and mentoring with Peg!

3. Create your own custom *Freedom Makeover Program* that can include:
   - Private VIP Day
   - Online Coaching Programs
   - Private 1:1 Coaching in person or online
   - Peg's Signature <u>11-Day Jump Start Delicious Detox Program</u>;
   - Peg's Signature 28-Day Freedom Through Food Plant-Based Transformation Program
   - Invitation to the "Fear To Freedom" Community Facebook Forum

A free 30-minute phone consultation is available to learn what next step is right for you. Please visit <u>www.FearToFreedom.com</u> or call (315) 398-1989

You will escape your anxiety prison and enjoy life as it was meant to be lived.

It's time to rise and shine!

Further Reading/Resources

Freedom For Your Mind

Kabat-Zinn, Jon. 1994. *Wherever You Go, There You Are*. New York: Hyperion.

Robbins, Anthony. 1986. *Unlimited Power*. New York: Free Press.

Robbins, Anthony. 1991. *Awaken the Giant Within*. New York: Free Press.

Freedom For Your Body

Beck, Judith. 2008. *The Beck Diet Solution*. Birmingham, A.L.: Oxmoor House Inc.

Robbins, John. 1987. *Diet for a New America*. Walpole, N.H.: Stillpoint Publishing.

Rosenthal, Joshua. 2007. *Integrative Nutrition*. New York: Greenleaf Book Group LLC.

Ross, Julia, 2002. *The Mood Cure*. New York: Penguin Books.

Sroufe, Del. *Forks Over Knives—The Cookbook*. 2012. New York: The Experiment LLC.

Basic Yoga Workout for Dummies. 2001. Anchor Bay Entertainment. DVD.

Freedom For *You!*

Chopra, Deepak. 1994. *The Seven Spiritual Laws of Success.* San Rafael, Calif.: New World Library.

Dyer, Wayne. 2001. *10 Secrets for Success and Inner Peace.* Carlsbad, Calif.: Hay House Inc.

Dyer, Wayne. 2004. *The Power of Intention.* Carlsbad, Calif.: Hay House, Inc.

Dyer, Wayne. 2010. *The Shift.* Carlsbad, Calif.: Hay House, Inc.

Madanes, Cloe. 2009. *Relationship Breakthrough.* New York: Rodale Inc.

Norwood, Robin. 1985. *Women Who Love Too Much: When You Keep Wishing and Hoping He'll Change.* New York: Pocket Books.

Tolle, Eckhart. 1997. *The Power of Now.* Novato, Calif.: New World Library.

Tolle, Eckhart. 2005. *A New Earth.* New York: Plume.

Williamson, Marianne. 1996. *A Return to Love: Reflections on the Principles of a "Course in Miracles."* New York: HarperCollins Publishers.

Zukav, Gary. 1990. *The Seat of the Soul.* New York: Fireside Books.

About the Author

Peg Haust-Arliss, LCSW-R, is a licensed clinical social worker, certified cognitive therapist, strategic interventionist, relationship educator, NLP practitioner and vegan health and lifestyle Coach. She has achieved additional certifications and trainings related to trauma, domestic violence and sexual assault. She holds active memberships in NASW, ACT, and AADP.

Peg's own struggle with anxiety disorder led her be to the specialist she is today. She has been counseling, guiding, and empowering others for nearly two decades to break out of imprisoning fears and break through to personal freedom.

Peg's experience and ongoing educational pursuits underscore her appreciation for learning and her dedication to providing her clients with the best and highest quality services. She received her master's degree from Syracuse University and has had the honor and privilege of learning from masters in her field. She personally trained with world-renowned psychotherapists, Cloe Madanes and the Becks at The Beck Institute of Cognitive Therapy. She trained again with Cloe Madanes at the Robbins-Madanes Institute for Strategic Intervention, learning from coaching genius Anthony Robbins and Mark and Magali Peysha. Her latest training with Dr. Matthew B. James, president of The Empowerment Partnership, earned her certification as a neuro-linguistic programming (NLP) practitioner.

Peg knows that psychology is a vital part of emotional wellness, and she knows it's not enough. Nurturing one's health, body, and spirit is an absolute necessity to achieve and maintain optimal and lasting results. For that reason, she also graduated from the Institute for Integrative Nutrition and became a board-certified health coach. Specializing in plant-based vegan living, she also completed studies at the Vegetarian Health Institute.

Peg jokes of her ever-growing list of certifications and what she really wants to accomplish:

"Yes, I might have a slight addiction to growth and learning. I've accepted it! And I know it's not the most important criteria for some people in choosing a therapist or coach. People just want to feel better and they deserve to! I love people, and it saddens me to see others feeling unfulfilled. This not only affects them, but everyone around them. I see people unhappy in relationships, feeling tired and stressed, selling themselves short, and giving up on dreams. I was there! They don't realize, and neither did I, that they already have everything they need. That's what I do best! First, I educate. I help people become aware of their thought-mood connection, identify their mental, emotional, and physical junk. Then I teach them to clear away that garbage that's been preventing optimal happiness and health. Next, I give them the tools and strategies they need to enrich and feed their own rich nutrient soil of their mind, body, and soul. I want people to clearly know that no matter what their age or current circumstances, they can own their life!"

Professionally, Peg is the proud owner of Fear To Freedom Holistic Psychotherapy. Her thriving private practice is located in the beautiful Finger Lakes area of upstate NY, where she offers in-person and online individual therapy, VIP Day Breakthrough Sessions, and coaching programs based on her book. She also offers education and coaching for plant-based vegan living.

Personally, Peg resides with her awesome husband and their four very adored and entertaining fur kids. She is passionate about animal advocacy and is on the board of ARAUNY, the Animal Rights Advocates of Upstate NY. For fun and relaxation she loves cooking, physical fitness, music, time with friends, wine touring, spa days, walking the dogs, very amateur photography, and spoiling her husband and loved ones any chance she gets!

Appendix Worksheets:

Point A: Life on the Inside; "Mug Shot" Assessment

All prisoners have a mug shot, right? Consider this yours. This is your Point A, where you are now. This is about everything you are currently struggling with. You will use this same tool to assess your midpoint and end results, so I suggest you print out three copies before you write on the original. Filling out this assessment may or may not create more feelings of anxiety in you. This is normal, and don't be afraid. It's only because as you are filling out the form, you are focusing on your problem. If you are focused on your problem, it's natural for you to *feel* that problem. Feel free to share this assessment with your primary care doctor or other health professionals. Remember, it is very important to rule out medical causes first, and this assessment tool can be incorporated into your existing care plan. My advice: be honest! You may not like some of your answers, and you may be tempted to soften them, but the truth shall set you free! Remember, you will be reassessing again at midpoint and again at the end, and you will want to celebrate your progress! Use this worksheet to answer the following questions.

Body

In this category the focus is on identifying physiological sensations that may occur during anxiety, the nourishment you're giving your body, your physical activity level, and the quality of sleep and relaxation your body is getting.

Panic/Anxiety Inventory
Below is a list of some common physiological sensations that occur during an anxiety or panic state. Please check all that apply during an anxious time.

____Shakiness
____Diarrhea
____Difficulty breathing or shortness of breath
____Nausea
____Hands trembling
____Abdominal distress/pain
____Rapid or pounding heart
____ Muscle tension
____ Numbness/tingling
____ Headaches
____ Hot flashes
____ Sweating
____ Unsteadiness or dizziness
____ Choking feeling
____ Other: _____

On average, how many times do you experience panic attacks in a week? _____ Last week?_____

How long do they last, generally?_____

How much do they bother you? Circle one:

Mildly   Moderately   Severely

Does anxiety cause you to avoid certain events or situations? Have you passed up opportunities because of it? If so, please list and explain.

Are you experiencing feelings of sadness, depression, or hopelessness?

If so, how would you rate the intensity of these feelings on a scale of 0–10, where 0=none and 10=the most severe unsafe/suicidal thoughts?

If you are experiencing intense feelings of depression and are feeling unsafe with yourself or having intentional thoughts of suicide, please get help now by calling 911, who will assist in connecting you with your local lifeline or mental health emergency services.

How is your energy level on an average day? Circle one.

Great   I have energy throughout the day without caffeine.

Good   A little slow in the morning and midafternoon, but I don't need caffeine.

Fair   I usually need a morning and midafternoon caffeine fix.

Poor   I live on caffeine and energy drinks to function.

Food and Substances

Caffeine: What and how much? Besides coffee, don't forget to include unexpected or often forgotten sources, like chocolate, tea, medications, energy drinks, and energy shots.

Alcohol: How many alcoholic beverages do you consume in a day/week, on average?

Medication: Are you taking any psychotropic meds for anxiety or depression? Please list type, dose, and start date.

Do not change or discontinue any medication regimen without consulting your health care professional.

Daily Meals

Please write out your typical daily meal regimen in detail. Write "none" if applicable.

Breakfast:

Midmorning snack:

Lunch:

Midafternoon snack:

Dinner:

Evening snack:

Supplements:

Herbal remedies:

How much plain water (lemon added okay) do you consume in a day?

Do you binge eat?

How many days of the week do you eat fast food?

How often do you consume foods high in sugar and/or preservatives?

    Circle: Daily   Weekly   Rarely

Have you ever been diagnosed with or do you have symptoms of IBS (irritable bowel syndrome)? (This is common with chronic anxiety sufferers.)

Sleep

    Total hours per night, on average:

Bedtime: Waking time:

Trouble falling asleep?   Y   N   Sometimes # Nights per week_____

Trouble staying asleep?   Y   N   Sometimes # Nights per week_____

Nightmares?   Y   N   Sometimes # Nights per week_____

Overall quality of sleep: Good   Fair   Poor

Movement

Do you participate in any form of physical exercise?

How often? _____days out of seven, for _____minutes a day.

Mind-set

In this category, the focus is on thoughts, perceptions, and beliefs. Please rate each statement 0–10, with 0 being the least true of you and 10 being absolutely true of you. Answer with your first gut-level response:

____ I tend to be a worrier.

____ I tend to take things personally; I'm pretty sensitive.

____ What if! What if! What if!

____ I have to admit, I'm a pretty negative thinker.

____ I've always been an anxious person.

____I've always been a shy person.

____I worry what others think of me.

____I often think I don't measure up; I'm not good enough or smart enough.

____ I imagine the worst-case scenario in many situations.

____I am a perfectionist.

____I am a people pleaser.

____Feeling certain, having a routine, and knowing the plan all sound really good.

____I get bored easily.

____I'm easily stressed over everyday common life challenges (hectic days, etc.).

____It's important to be successful in whatever I do.

____It's easy for me to love and trust people.

In the next exercise, think about what you want from life. If you are not where you want to be in your life right now, what do you think prevents you from having the life you want? Check all that apply:

____ Panic or anxiety challenge

____ Low self-confidence

____ Fear of change

____Fear of success

____ Fear of failure

____Fear of rejection

____Fear of disappointing others

____ Lack of time

____ Lack of motivation

____Disorganization

____Feeling overwhelmed

____Other people

____Depression

____Fear of disapproval

____ Situations beyond my control

____Relationship concerns

____Money issues

____Other:

Spirit

Here you are going to look at how you feed your spirit: the quality of your relationships, the stability of your environment, personal growth, and contribution. For now just reflect on your current situations.

Do you have a spiritual or religious belief? _____ If so, are you happy with the amount of time you commit to it?

Are you in an intimate relationship?

If so, how satisfied are you in the relationship? Please rate 0–10, with 0 meaning "I'm out of here!" and 10 meaning "I am happy and fulfilled!"

Domestic violence: Do you feel safe emotionally and physically in this relationship?

Is your partner understanding and supportive when it comes to your anxiety challenges?

What about other relationships? Do you have a support network of family and friends?

Do you work inside or outside the home? If so, please rate job satisfaction 0–10, with 0 meaning "I need out!" and 10 meaning "I couldn't be happier!"

Do you have interests or hobbies outside of work?

Do you volunteer?

If retired, how has your life changed for the better or worse?

Is there financial stress, health-related stress, or any extraordinary stressor in your life right now? If so, what?

Do you have children?

Do you have pets?

Do you feel fulfilled? If not, then what do you believe is missing? What do you think you need to feel fulfilled?

Point B: Life on the Outside; Your Freedom Awaits!

Have you ever thought about what you would do if only you were not challenged by excessive anxiety, panic, frustration, procrastination, or low confidence? This will take some time and thought, but *do not skip this step!* Whereas point A is your "before pic," this is your Point B, or your "after pic." These are the results you want to achieve and why you want to achieve them. This is your life outside of Anxiety Prison. I cannot stress enough how important this step is! Without this step you will not get the results you seek, because not knowing what you want and why you want it will make you quit when it gets uncomfortable; you will put this program on the shelf to collect dust, and create a story about why it didn't work for you. I am not going to let you do that! It's time to …

Identify Your Freedom!

What **exactly do I want?** Give yourself this gift. Grab a cup of chamomile tea, get your journal, and take some time now to write about what it is you want. When was the last time someone asked you, or when was the last time you asked yourself: *What do I really want for my life? What would I do, what would I be, what would I accomplish if this anxiety challenge was gone. If I had all the courage I needed, if fear was not a factor, what would be different? How would I feel differently? How would I behave differently? What opportunities would I take or seek out? What does freedom from anxiety look like for me?* I can't tell you how many people I have talked with who tell me what they want to be, do, or have—and then they immediately shift to all the reasons why they can't have them. And here's the thing—just like my experience, they think their dreams are too big! But, the truth is their desires aren't extraordinary! It's just their fear talking. What do *your* fears keep you from? Do you dream of having a wonderful relationship full of passion and love? Do you dream of owning your own home? Do you dream of starting a business offering something you love? Do you dream of writing a book? Do you want to go back to school? These are just some of the things I often hear people would love to do "if they only could." Take some time to write about what you want. It's your turn. Dare to dream!

What do I want? If anxiety was not a challenge I would …

_____

_____

_____

_____

_____

_____

_____

_____

_____

_____

_____

Why do I want it? Now that you know *what* you want, even more important is to know *why* you want it. You have committed to doing the work in this book. Why? Why are you putting in the effort? What are you doing this all for? Getting really clear on this will get you through the most challenging times. This is true for any dream, goal, or desire. Moving away from pain will motivate you to do this work, but it will only work in the short-term. With a big enough *why* you will find a way, because this will move you continuously forward. So ask yourself, *Why do I want what I want? What will it mean for me? What will it mean for those I love? What could it mean for others? How could I make a difference to the world if I fulfilled my dreams? How does this relate to my purpose?*

Why do I want that? Having or accomplishing all that I want would mean ...

_____

_____

_____

_____

_____

_____

_____

_____

_____

_____

_____.

You know that you have completed this part of the exercise in the most beneficial way when you can say: "That's it! This anxiety problem has to go _now_!"

Here is an example of how one client completed both parts of this exercise for herself. Notice how clear and specific her wants are and how her _why_ has the emotional charge necessary.

What do I want? If anxiety was not a challenge, I would ...
If anxiety was not a challenge, I would go for my biggest goal in my life: return to school to become a registered nurse. I would travel and eventually become a traveling RN! I would attract a loving, committed relationship that I have as yet only been wishing for. I would find a way to become completely financially independent. After pursuing my first passion, nursing, later in life I would become a hairstylist and makeup artist part-time.

Why do I want that?
Accomplishing that would mean I would become more self-fulfilled and happy! I would have so much confidence! I would be able to help

people out of the goodness of my heart, no matter what. With anxiety out of the way, I could do that! Dad has been such an inspiration for beating cancer time and time again, and my mother works hard with her many health issues present. If I was a nurse, I could contribute so much for them. Not to mention all the people who will need me and who I will serve as a nurse. Not just the patients, but their loved ones too! I would have opportunities to make new friends and be a friend—friends that I might not ever meet if I don't pursue my dreams. *And* if I was debt-free, I would be able to repay my parents for all that they have done for me and help them for what they are going through. As for fulfilling my artistic goals in life, I will be free to express my creative side! I had many opportunities working with my friends that are hairstylists. I will be able to help others feel beautiful inside (as a nurse) and out! And with anxiety out of my way, I just might realize that I have the greatest qualities to offer someone, and settling for something that is less than what I deserve won't be happening. All in all, making a difference in someone's life, now and in the future, will be truly amazing!

Now that you specifically know what you want and realize there is no option but to have it, how are you going to get out of your own way to get it? There are three keys that—when used together—will unlock the door to your anxiety prison and set you free for life. I am sharing them in the order in which I received them for myself. I didn't obtain them all at once. I wish I had, because I would have gained the long-term benefits sooner. I am grateful I have all the keys now and that I can share them with you all at once!

Commitment Statement

> "Every failure, obstacle or hardship is an opportunity in disguise. The greatest pollution problem we face today is negativity. Believe you can do anything. Replace 'If I can, I hope, maybe' with 'I can, I will, I must.'"
>
> —Mary Kay Ash

I, _____, commit to the following:

1.

2.

3.

4.

5.

6.

7.

8.

9.

10.

11.

Signed_____Date_____

Getaway C-A-R Worksheet (Blank)

Whenever you notice your anxiety speeding up, remember you have the brake. STOP and breathe. Shake off any excess energy. This worksheet will train you to CATCH the low octane thoughts, ANALYZE for accuracy and then REFUEL, resulting in a new high-performance vehicle. With practice you will soon be on auto-drive. You will see two possible outcomes:

1. You will realize that you are creating your anxious response unnecessarily and be able to change or decrease the intensity of your anxious state.
   OR
2. You will realize that what you are feeling is accurate, and instead of going into old emotional patterns, you will focus on solutions and take action.

Either way, once you realize that YOU are behind the wheel of your emotions, imagine how far you will go! Use this worksheet when you are experiencing or reflecting upon a situation that leads you to experience a distressing emotion.

Emotional State:
What are/were you feeling? Rate Intensity 0-10

Neutral Event:
Identify the situation, event, thought, memory, or image leading to the emotion listed above.

Step #1 CATCH: List the automatic thoughts, assumptions, meanings and/or beliefs that you were thinking just before you began to feel the emotion. Underline any power language: words, phrases, questions that triggered or increased the intensity of the emotional state.

Step #2 ANALYZE: Time for a test drive. Look at your thoughts above and answer the questions below that are applicable:

1. Can I say with 100 percent certainty that it is true?

2. What else could it mean? What else is possible?

3. Could I be misjudging, misperceiving, mishearing, or misunderstanding the situation or person?

4. Am I forgetting to remember anything about the situation or person that would make a difference?

5. If I took myself out of the situation and looked in as an observer, what would I see differently?

6. Am I looking at this through the lens of FEAR? What happens when I change the lens to LOVE?

7. If I eliminate or change any power language, does that change how I feel?

8. Take each thought and write the complete opposite. How does that feel?

9. What can I be grateful for now? Where's the gift in this situation?

Step #3 REFUEL: Choose one outcome below and proceed to refuel for a new result.

Outcome #1
After completing STEP 2 I am able to identify a new perspective or meaning regarding the neutral event: Did that trigger a new emotional state or lessen the existing one? Emotional State: Rate Intensity 0-10

OR

Outcome #2
After completing STEP 2 I conclude that my initial emotion is on target. Now ask yourself:

1. What is the emotion's purpose for me? How is it trying to help me?

2. What emotional state would serve me best in this situation? How would I need to feel to be most effective and less affected? Courageous? Confident? Calm?

3. What can I do now to address the issue? What can I do now to get myself into the empowering state listed above?

4. What resources do I have and what do I need to take action?

5. How can I best take care of myself during this difficult time? Who needs me right now too?

NEW AWARENESS, INSIGHTS AND CONCLUSIONS

Getaway C-A-R Worksheet
(Client's Example with Outcome #1)

Emotional State:
What are/were you feeling? *Anxious* Rate Intensity 0-10 **8**

Neutral Event:
Identify the situation, event, memory, or image leading to the emotion stated above.
Thinking about having to fly next week when we leave for vacation

Step #1 CATCH: List the automatic thoughts/images, assumptions, meanings and/or beliefs that you were thinking just before you began to feel the emotion. Underline any power language: words, phrases, or questions that triggered or intensified the emotional state.

"<u>OMG</u>, I am <u>never going to be able to get on that plane!</u>" "<u>What if</u> I have a panic attack?" "<u>What's wrong with me?</u>" "I am <u>never</u> going to get over this." "People are going to notice and I will be <u>completely humiliated</u>." IMAGE: I can see myself <u>completely mortified</u> after having a panic attack on the plane. Meaning: Plane flights are dangerous.

Step #2 ANALYZE: Time for a test drive. Look at your thoughts above and answer the questions below that are applicable:

1. Can I say with 100 percent certainty that it is true? *No.*
2. What else could it mean? What else is possible? *I could look at it as a great practice opportunity. And it's possible I will get through it.*
3. Could I be misjudging, misperceiving, mishearing, or misunderstanding the situation or person? *I am clearly catastrophizing, focusing on the worst-case scenario!*
4. Am I forgetting to remember anything about the situation or person that would make a difference? **Yes, I am forgetting**

that plane flying is still safer than driving according to statistics and there are way more flights that are just boring flights. Hey BORING is a good word to use!

5. If I took myself out of the situation and looked in as an observer, what would I see differently? **From an observer perspective I might notice that there are other people who might be nervous too, and I could help them by striking up a conversation.**

6. Am I looking at this through the lens of FEAR? What happens when I change the lens to LOVE? *YES, FEAR! Looking through the lens of LOVE I see very understanding people who will help me not judge myself even if I did freak out.*

7. If I eliminate or change any power language, does that change how I feel? *Yes, not using words like humiliated, mortified, and OMG decreases the intensity greatly.*

8. Take each thought and write the complete opposite. How does that feel?
OMG I got on the plane! Yeah me! What if I don't have a panic attack? What's right with me? I am definitely going to get over this! People are not going to notice. IMAGE: I now see myself smiling and enjoying the plane flight.

9. What could I be grateful for in this situation? Where's the gift?

I am SO grateful I have the money to fly at all! I am SO grateful I have family to visit somewhere warm! I am SO grateful for the time saved by flying. I am SO grateful for the time off to take the trip.

Step #3 REFUEL Using Outcome #1:
After analyzing for accuracy I am able to identify a new perspective or meaning regarding the neutral event:
I was giving the plane flight the meaning of danger, and so my fight or flight response naturally kicked in. I changed my perspective to 'plane flying is safe and actually BORING!'

Did that trigger a new emotional state or lessen the existing one? *New* Emotional State: **Just A little nervous** Rate Intensity 0-10 **4**

NEW AWARENESS, INSIGHTS, AND CONCLUSIONS: *Yes, I realize how I literally work myself up into an anxious state.* I went from an 8-level anxiety state to a just a little nervous! *I noticed that I use power language that gets me in trouble. I will watch my words! I love calling plane flights boring! I also love the idea of looking through the lens of Love and the Observer. If I do have a panic attack, then I will get through it, but I am not in danger. Yes, plane flights can be dangerous, but I can't live my life in fear! And remembering gratitude is an instant mood shifter!*

Getaway C-A-R Worksheet
(Client's Example with Outcome #2)

Emotional State:
What are/were you feeling? **Overwhelmed** Rate Intensity 0-10 **8**

Neutral Event:
Identify the situation, event, memory, or image leading to the emotion stated above: *Thinking about all the things I have to do in my life.*

Step #1 CATCH: List the automatic thoughts/images, assumptions, meanings and/or beliefs that you were thinking just before you began to feel the emotion. Underline any power language: words, phrases, or questions that triggered or intensified the emotional state. *"There is <u>SO</u> much I <u>have to</u> do." "I'll <u>never</u> make that deadline at work." "I don't have time." "People don't help!" Image: I picture myself stepping over laundry and dishes piling up. I picture running late to work.*

Step #2 ANALYZE: Time for a test drive. Look at your thoughts above and answer the questions below that are applicable:

1. Can I say with 100 percent certainty that it is true? **It's true I have much going on, but not all my thoughts are 100 percent certain.**
2. What else could it mean? What else is possible?
3. Could I be misjudging, misperceiving, mishearing, or misunderstanding the situation or person?
4. Am I forgetting to remember anything about the situation or person that would make a difference?
    Everyone has the same hours in a day. I know people who manage time well.
5. If I took myself out of the situation and looked in as an observer. What would I see differently?

I see that I am not taking time out and it's building too much stress. I realize that I really do need to slow down!

6. Am I looking at this through the lens of FEAR? What happens when I change the lens to LOVE?
FEAR, because I am afraid of not getting things done. If I don't get things done I will fail. If I looked through lens of Love, I would be kinder to myself and more understanding of others who I get mad at for not helping me. They are overwhelmed too.

7. If I eliminate or change any power language does that change how I feel? **Using words like NEVER and EVERYTHING intensifies the state. Peg taught me to use "I get to" instead of "I have to." That helps so much!**

8. Take each thought and write the complete opposite. How does that feel? *There is little to do. I will make that deadline at work. I have all the time I need. People are helpful. I picture myself doing all I need to do without stressing. I see the end result of a clean house and work projects complete.*

9. What can I be grateful for now? What's the gift in this situation? *I am grateful that I GET TO go to work, I have a busy life, but I GET TO live it!*

Step #3 REFUEL Using Outcome #2:

After completing STEP 2 I conclude that the initial emotion is on target: **It makes sense that I** *feel overwhelmed.* If yes, ask yourself:

1. What is the emotion's purpose for me? How is it trying to help me? *The purpose of overwhelm is to tell me I need to take something off my plate or prioritize my projects.*

2. What emotional state would serve me best in this situation? How would I need to feel to be most effective and less affected? *Calm determination is how I want to feel!*

3. What can I do now to address the issue? What can I do now to get myself into the empowering state listed above? *Practice focus! Focus on one thing at a time and being in the present moment as I do things.*
4. What resources do I have and what do I need to take action? *All I need is within me now! I also have a supportive spouse who can help if I really need him to help with the chores. I have a supervisor who I can talk to if I need work support.*
5. How can I best take care of myself during this difficult time? Who needs me right now too? *I will make sure I take time out for me and my family on the weekends. I will take mini breaks to just breathe at work. I will eat well and get to bed early.*

NEW AWARENESS, INSIGHTS AND CONCLUSIONS: I think I am actually in the habit of rushing even when I am not late. That was a big realization! I need to break this habit by consciously slowing down and mindfully focusing on one thing at a time. I can get myself into a state of calm determination, and with consistency that will become my new habit.